HOLD THAT HIDDEN SALT!

To all my recipe testers (roommates, family, co-workers) thank you for seeing this cookbook and recipes through the good and not-so-good times to the finished product. Mom, again a special thanks to you. Testing recipes is much more enjoyable in good company.

To my good friend Craig Flinn: without your brilliant suggestions and expertise several of these recipes would have never made the final cut. A BIG thanks to Michael Howell for once again making my recipes look so fabulous for this cookbook and for all your helpful tips and suggestions. Jennifer Partridge, you have an eye for detail. Thank you for capturing such beautiful pictures.

To all the staff at Formac, thank you for all your hard work, support and guidance.

Photography Including cover image by Jennifer Partridge, except the following: IStock - 6; 8; 9; 12; 19; 23; 27; 34; 39; 43; 45; 73; 81; 83; 84; 85; 87; 92; 95; 96; 127; 137

Formac Publishing Company Limited recognizes the support of the Province of Nova Scotia through the Department of Tourism, Culture and Heritage. We acknowledge the financial support of the Government of Canada through the Canada Book Fund for our publishing activities.

NOVA SCOTIA
Tourism, Culture and Heritage   Canadä

Library and Archives Canada Cataloguing in Publication

Tilley, Maureen
        Hold that hidden salt : Recipes for delicious alternatives to processed, salt-heavy supermarket favourites / Maureen Tilley.

Issued also in an electronic format.
ISBN 978-0-88780-952-1

        1. Salt-free diet—Recipes. 2. Hypertension—Diet therapy—Recipes.
3. Quick and easy cookery. I. Title.

RM237.8.T55 2010   641.5'6323   C2010-902641-1

Formac Publishing Company Limited
5502 Atlantic Street
Halifax, Nova Scotia, Canada B3H 1G4
www.formac.ca

Printed and bound in China

HOLD THAT HIDDEN SALT!

RECIPES FOR DELICIOUS ALTERNATIVES TO PROCESSED, SALT-HEAVY SUPERMARKET FAVOURITES

MAUREEN TILLEY

FORMAC PUBLISHING COMPANY LIMITED
HALIFAX

Contents

You're at the grocery store trying to decide what to pick up . . .

for your meals and snacks for the week. You need quick and convenient foods to fit your hectic lifestyle — or perhaps you have neither the skills nor the time to prepare meals from scratch. You zip through the frozen food section and down the aisles, grabbing frozen dinners, boxed cereal, frozen pizza, bread and frozen burgers. Perhaps you do prepare some meals so you pick up a bottle of tomato sauce for spaghetti, teriyaki sauce for a stir-fry and chicken broth for soup. These products certainly cut back your time in the kitchen but not without a cost to your health and your blood pressure, because they're laced with sodium.

Why is there so much sodium in food?

The food industry adds salt mainly because salt tastes good and it's cheap. It's unfortunate: consumers demand the taste of salt, industry cuts costs and health takes the back burner.

How do you know if foods are too high in salt?

First, know that your taste buds are not the best indicators. The taste of salt in high-sodium foods can be masked by other flavours, such as sugar. A commercial muffin, for example, contains over half the sodium recommended for an entire day. If you regularly add salt, consume convenience foods or often eat out at restaurants, your taste buds have likely become accustomed to the taste of salt and you won't notice how much you're getting in the food. Your best sodium indicators are the ingredient list, the nutrition claims and the nutrition fact label, and how much salt you see added during cooking or at the table.

Adding salt while you are cooking or to your plate

A pinch there, a pinch here . . . there's no harm in just a pinch, right? Unfortunately, wrong! It doesn't take much to reach the daily sodium recommendation and adding extra to your food probably means you're getting too much sodium in your diet. The proper thing to do is to cook from scratch and omit salt from your recipes and at the table. Cut it back slowly and you won't even notice the change.

The ingredient list

The ingredients are always listed according to quantity so the higher an item is on the list, the more of it there is in the product. Sodium is a mineral of many names, but whether they call it Na, sodium, monosodium glutamate/ MSG, sodium sulphite, disodium phosphate or sodium citrate, it's still salt.

Nutritional claims

Packaging that states "Low in sodium" and "No added salt" means that the product contains an acceptable level of sodium. "Reduced sodium" means that it contains 25 per cent less sodium than a previous version. Be careful, though; read the label. The 75 per cent that remains can still be too much.

The nutrition fact label

When you read a label, check the serving size first. Is it a realistic serving? Next, look at the %Daily Value (%DV). This value is based on 2300 to 2400 mg of sodium. It's likely you require less than this, so choose the foods with the lowest %DV per serving size. Ideally, it's best to aim for values closest to 5%DV and never to accept anything over 10%DV.

Which foods are high in salt?

The main source of sodium for most people is prepared and packaged food.

The main culprits include:	The sneaky ones include:
• Frozen and ready-to-eat meals • Pizza • Hamburgers • Cheese • Deli and processed meats • Prepared soups and broths • Snack foods like pretzels, chips, nachos and peanuts • Restaurant meals and fast food	• Condiments like ketchup, mustard, relish and mayonnaise • Pancakes • Muffins • Tomato and alfredo sauces • Breads • Seasoned meats such as chicken and pork • Cereals • Vegetable and tomato juices

How much salt is good? How much is too much?

Chances are you have this book in your hands because you know already that salt can cause health problems, and that keeping down the salt you and your family eat is good for you. You may think that the price of using less salt will be that your food won't be tasty — but that's not true at all, as I hope you'll find out by trying the recipes here. Chances are, too, that you know that most of the salt that most of us eat comes from packaged foods and restaurant foods — not from the food we prepare at home. My previous book, *Hold the Salt!*, offered a variety of recipes for home-cooked meals using less salt. This book tackles the more difficult and more important kind of salt — the salt we all get from packaged and restaurant foods.

The first question is how much salt is too much? I think you'll be surprised by the answer, and by how hard that answer is to find.

First, the answer. The Daily Recommended Intake (DRI) of sodium for an average adult is 1,500 mg. Observing this level is especially important for individuals with or at risk for high blood pressure. The Upper Tolerable Limit (UL) for healthy adults is 2,300 mg a day. New Canadian government standards state that, ideally, every adult should aim for 1,500 mg a day and individuals who exceed 2,300 mg are at risk for health complications. But note that the recommendations vary according to age.

Where do these Daily Recommended Intakes come from? They are set out on Health Canada's website, where they're described as "a comprehensive set of nutrient

Daily Recommended Sodium Intake by Age

* There is no recommended level for children under the age of 1, but prepared foods for infants often have surprisingly high levels of sodium.

"I can have 1,000 mg." Ages 1 to 3

"I can have 1,200 mg." Ages 4 to 8

"I can have 1,500 mg." Ages 9 to 50

"I can have 1,300 mg." Ages 51 to 70

"I can have 1,200 mg." Ages 70+

Source: www.statcan.gc.ca/pub/82-003-x/2006004/article/sodium/4148995-sodium/4148995-eng.htm

reference values for healthy populations that can be used for assessing and planning diets." They were drawn up by a group of Canadian and American scientists and reviewed under the U.S. National Academies, which is an independent, authoritative, nongovernmental group.

Reading the labels: reader beware!

If you're thinking that it's pretty simple to find out how much salt is too much, even if the amounts do vary depending on age, you're right. But food manufacturers have other ideas. They have decided to — and so far they are being allowed to do this — calculate their labels on the assumption that the recommended daily sodium amount is not 1,500 mg, but 2,400. Notice this — 2,400 mg a day exceeds the recommended daily amount by 900 mg, or 60 per cent! This makes quite a difference. If you were to see that a 50 g portion of potato chips (not a large amount) with its 750 mg of sodium accounts for 50 per cent of the recommended daily sodium amount for an average adult, you would be a lot more worried than if the label on the product tells you it's "only" 31 per cent. Today, the label will tell you it's 31 per cent. But I would say that 50 per cent would be a more reliable number for those potato chips.

In the pages to come, we've shown the nutritional analysis as it appears on the packages for the products we selected, but we've added our own calculation of the sodium amount based on the 1,500-mg level. We've calculated the sodium levels for our own recipes the same way, to make the comparison fair.

If you're wondering how the food manufacturers justify using 2,400 mg as the base for their calculations, I think their answer would be that 2,400 (actually 2,300) is the Tolerable Limit for adults. But I wouldn't recommend that anyone treat either 2,400 or 2,300 as an acceptable amount — and certainly not anyone who has or is at risk of high blood pressure, strokes, heart attacks, etc.

One more warning if you rely on product labels to tell you about salt and sodium: the amounts shown are based on an arbitrary portion size. The label does tell you what the portion size is — for instance, for prepared mustard it is often 1 tsp. For some cereals it may be 1/4 cup. Often the portion size is unrealistically small, though, and you will find you and your family normally eat several times the label portion size. If 1 tsp of mustard has 150 mg of sodium, and you use 4 tsp worth on your hot dog, you've just had 600 mg of sodium — and that's not counting the hot dog itself, let alone the bun. I have noticed that many manufacturers of high-salt items use small portion sizes as a way of minimizing the amount of salt their products seem to contain. So — be aware, and be wary!

How many people eat too much salt?

Perhaps one reason there hasn't been more controversy about the way manufacturers calculate recommended daily amounts of salt and sodium is that most people consume far more than they should, far more even than the 2,300 mg or 2,400 mg, let alone the 1,500 mg. According to the Canadian Medical Association, the average sodium intake of Canadians is 3,400 mg a day. In fact, 97 per cent of children and teens, 83 per cent of Canadian women and 85 per cent of Canadian men eat enough sodium to put them at risk for health complications and disease. So the emphasis now is simply on getting people to eat much less salt, and for good reason. Most people do not recognize the toll sodium takes on our health. Researchers have calculated that 30 to 40 deaths a day could be prevented if Canadians followed the daily sodium recommendation!

The Canadian government is taking action with its Sodium Reduction Strategy. The goal is to promote a standard of 1,500 mg of sodium a day and to reduce the average Canadian sodium intake to 2,300 mg by 2016. Pressure is being put on the food and restaurant industry to cut back the sodium in their foods and to make the nutritional information on their products more accessible. But, as many newspaper editorials have pointed out, progress to date has been painfully slow. And the salt-reduction targets agreed to so far by the manufacturers of processed foods have been modest indeed.

We can't rely solely on government initiatives. We do need to advocate for reduced-sodium foods — but also, as individuals, we can and should take responsibility for our own dietary choices and health. We can hold the hidden salt — and this is the book that shows how!

What does reducing salt do for you?

If your doctor or health professional tells you to cut back on salt, your first reaction is probably "My food won't taste good." Hopefully, you'll try these recipes and discover for yourself that you can hold the salt and still get great-tasting meals.

But the real reason for reducing salt is that it's good for your health. A great many Canadians are at risk of high blood pressure, and that is associated with strokes and heart attacks. Millions of people take drugs every day to bring down their blood pressure. That's good for the drug companies, and it's good for the health of the people on drugs. But often the problem has started with — you've guessed it — too much salt! Reduce the amount of salt in your diet, and you're reducing the likelihood of the problems arising. Reduce the amount of salt, and you can actually bring down your blood pressure. Read about the DASH diet, and you'll see that the combination of a moderate sodium intake and eating a wide range of fruits and vegetables has been proven to be just as effective as drugs in reducing hypertension. Reducing sodium has a range of other health benefits too.

Why so much salt?

Too much salt in our diets is good for only one thing: to generate profits. Profits for the companies that produce salt, and for the food manufacturers who add salt as a cheap way to preserve foods and to kick up the taste.

Manufacturers claim that they have to use lots of salt because their food is tasteless without it. Manufacturers have given legislators samples of familiar foods made without salt, to "prove" that they need salt to get those familiar flavours. What they don't say is that if they had to cut back on salt they would have to use better and more expensive ingredients — and that might not be good for profits. But in many other countries the transition to lower salt in manufactured items has been made. It could be done here too, if the government insisted on it.

Many people who are used to a lot of salt do find that food without salt is tasteless. But take my word for it: that happens only when you're used to too much salt in your food. Salt is an acquired taste! Cut back on processed foods with salt by trying these recipes instead, and you'll be pleasantly surprised by the tastes you experience. After a couple of weeks of moderate daily amounts of salt, you'll find that many of the items you used to find "normal" and "tasty" will seem excessively salty. That's because they *are* excessively salty! .

References:

Health Canada. "Dietary Reference Intakes." http://www.hc-sc.gc.ca/fn-an/nutrition/reference/index-eng.php.

Lauren Vogel. "Health Canada sidesteps commitment to new salt reduction strategy." Canadian Medical Association, CMAJ, doi: 10.1503/cmaj.109-3326, http://www.cmaj.ca/cgi/content/full/182/12/E571?maxtoshow=&hits=10&RESULTFORMAT=&fulltext=salt&searchid=1&FIRSTINDEX=0&sortspec=date&resourcetype=HWCIT.

Health Canada. *Sodium Reduction Strategy for Canada: Recommendations of the Sodium Working Group*. July, 2010. http://www.hc-sc.gc.ca/fn-an/alt_formats/pdf/nutrition/sodium/strateg/index-eng.pdf.

Watch our video clips to go behind-the-scenes with Chef Michael Howell and author Maureen Tilley! Look for this symbol next to your favourite recipes or check www.holdthesalt.ca/videos for a complete list.

What exactly is high blood pressure?

High blood pressure, also known as hypertension, affects 20 per cent of Canadians. It is a leading cause of heart disease and the number-one risk factor for stroke. Scarily enough, it is known as "the silent killer" because often it doesn't present with any symptoms. That explains why an estimated 43 per cent of people who have it don't know they have it. Hypertension occurs when there is stress put on the blood vessels, causing scarring and plaque build-up, interfering with the passage of blood to the heart, the brain and other parts of the body. If this disease is left untreated, it can result in weakening of the heart and can lead to bursting of a vessel in the brain, resulting in a stroke. In addition, hypertension can also lead to a number of diseases that affect the tissues and organs, including congestive heart failure, end-stage kidney disease and peripheral vascular disease (decreased blood flow to the legs and feet).

Blood pressure level is measured by systolic and diastolic pressure. Systolic measures the pressure on your heart as it beats when blood is being pushed out of the heart into the body. Diastolic measures the pressure on the heart between beats, when blood is flowing into the heart. High blood pressure is generally defined as a systolic blood pressure (SBP) of 140 mmHg or higher or a diastolic blood pressure (DBP) of 90 mmHg or higher, or both.

So you have concerns with high blood pressure. What can you do about it?

Lots! Prescription medications are effective in lowering blood pressure, but lifestyle changes are proven to be equally good. Eating healthy foods, in conjunction with regular physical activity, will benefit your overall health, your heart function and your blood pressure. Research shows that a healthy lifestyle can decrease or eliminate the need for blood pressure medications or even let you avoid taking them to begin with. It's important to always talk to your doctor prior to making any changes to your diet or medication.

The DASH diet — is it effective? Prove it!

The DASH diet, which stands for Dietary Approaches to Stop Hypertension, is a research-based approach to lowering blood pressure. The Canadian Heart & Stroke Foundation and the American Heart Association both endorse this diet. As a dietitian, I know that in the healthcare world this diet is highly supported and recommended. It is based on two studies, the DASH study and DASH-Sodium study, both of which looked at the effect of diet on blood pressure. In the DASH study, participants followed one of three diet regimes for an eight-week period:

Group A: a typical North American diet

Group B: North American diet with extra fruits and vegetables

Group C: DASH diet with emphasis on fruits and vegetables, whole grains, low-fat dairy products and minimized intake of sweets and red meat

The results were compelling. Participants from Group B and C showed a decrease in blood pressure and cholesterol compared to Group A. Group C (DASH diet) showed the most significant improvement in blood pressure. Within two weeks the diet was similar in effectiveness to taking blood pressure medication.

The DASH-Sodium study took a similar dietary approach but looked at the effect of sodium (salt) on blood pressure, as well. The participants were again divided into three groups:

Group A: a typical North American diet with a typical sodium intake of 3,300 mg/day

Group B: North American diet with extra fruits and vegetables, and moderately restricted sodium intake of 2,400 mg/day (~1 tsp/5 mL).

Group C: DASH diet with emphasis on fruit and vegetables, whole grains, low-fat dairy products, minimized intake of sweets and red meat and a restricted sodium intake of 1,500 mg/day (~2/3 tsp/3 mL).

As suspected, the results showed the negative effect sodium has on blood pressure. Group B and Group C had the most improvement in blood pressure and even better results than the equivalent groups in the DASH study. This provided further evidence to support the DASH diet with a sodium restriction.

The nitty gritty on the DASH diet

The main focus of the DASH diet is on fruits, vegetables, nuts, legumes, fish, whole grains and low-fat dairy products, while decreasing consumption of red meat, butter, high-fat foods and salt. The DASH diet is very similar to the recommendations of Canada's Food Guide but its serving sizes are more specific and it calls for more servings of fruits and vegetables.

The recommended servings for 2,000 to 2,100 daily calorie intakes are:

Food Group	DASH	Canada's Food Guide
Grains and grain products	6 to 8	6 to 8
Vegetables	4 to 5	7 to 10
Fruits	4 to 5	included with vegetables
Low-fat dairy products	2 to 3	2 to 3
Meat and alternatives	6 or less (1 oz each)	2 to 3 (2.5-oz/75-mg servings)
Fats	2 to 3 (1 oz each)	2 to 3 (1 tbsp, 15 mL)
Nuts, seeds and legumes	4 to 5 per week	included with meats
Sweets	5 per week	Not specified

Improving your lifestyle is all about making realistic and maintainable changes that work for you. Do not try to incorporate all the DASH recommendations at once, because that can be overwhelming and difficult to maintain in the long run. The trick is to set yourself up for success. Follow the tips below and you will be on your way to taking charge of your health.

• Watch your sodium intake. It's important not to exceed a daily sodium intake of 2,300 mg and ideally to aim for 1,500 mg/day. Keep in mind that most salt in your diet does not come from what you add at the table or while cooking, but from prepared foods, processed meats, condiments, sauces, snack foods, canned foods and restaurants.

• Increase your potassium intake. Potassium is a mineral that plays an important role in blood pressure control. It helps keep the water in our bodies balanced, and, in our blood vessels, that helps control blood pressure. The daily recommendation for those with hypertension is 4,700 mg. Many fruits and vegetables, dairy products, nuts and legumes are rich in potassium. Some high sources are bananas, potatoes, spinach, tomatoes, oranges, mushrooms, milk, lentils and almonds. You can take potassium in supplement form, but it is not proven to be as effective as when obtained from food.

• Eat a diet rich in antioxidants. Antioxidants are substances that eliminate and repair cell damage done to our bodies by harmful chemicals called free radicals. Research shows that damage from free radicals may play a role in the progression of certain diseases such as cancer, high blood pressure and heart disease. Fruits and vegetables are a rich source of antioxidants, and their colour is an indication of the level: the darker and richer the colour, the higher the antioxidant content. Just another reason to make sure you are eating plenty of fruits and vegetables.

• Start by incorporating one or two extra servings of fruit and vegetables sometime during your day and steadily increase that to the recommended daily intake.

• Gradually cut back on your salt intake to allow your taste buds to adjust.

• Decrease the use of high-fat foods and condiments (butter, margarine, milk and milk products) by lowering your portion size or by switching to low-fat and fat-free items or by doing both.

• Slowly cut back your meat portions by a third at each meal until you reach the recommended serving size, and aim to incorporate more vegetables at meals.

• Be vegetarian at least one day a week and enjoy more beans, lentils, nuts and other vegetarian items.

• Become label savvy and be aware of what's in your foods.

• Prepare more meals at home. You don't need a lot of time, just a little organization. This is the best way to control what goes into your food and into your mouth.

Controlling hypertension is essential to preventing and treating its possible side effects, which can include heart disease and stroke. Although there is no cure for hypertension, it can be prevented, and its symptoms can be managed through dietary and lifestyle changes. I'll say it once again: it's nearly impossible to find "convenience" meals that do not have a negative impact on our blood pressure and heart health. This book is intended to help you eat better, with quick recipes that are suitable for your fast-paced lifestyle and, most importantly, for your health. So, cheers to good food and improved health!

Enjoy!

Breakfast Foods and Breads

>muffins

No wonder muffins are so popular...

grabbing a muffin on the go in the morning or throughout the day makes a quick and tasty breakfast or snack. Most regard muffins as a healthy choice but, unfortunately, more often than not this is not the case.

In fact, most premade muffins are distinguished from cake only by the name.

Many are loaded with sugar and fat, but most alarming is the amount of salt. One Tim Horton's muffin has 770 mg of sodium!

To put this into perspective, that is one-half of the recommended 1,500 mg sodium for the entire day and for those with or at risk for hypertension. Even if you are a healthy adult, this is still one-third of the Canadian daily upper limit recommendation of 2,300 mg.

What about store-bought muffin mix? The Quaker muffin mix label shows sodium levels significantly lower than Tim Horton's — "only" 300 mg. But this is for a 38 g muffin; Tim Horton's is 128 g. Make that the same size muffin, and it turns out that there is less sodium in the Tim Horton's!

Fortunately, there is an easy, tasty, and relatively quick alternative — delicious homemade muffins made using a low-salt recipe. As an added bonus, these muffins also contain more fibre, more fruit, and fewer calories. Your health and taste buds will thank you!

HOLD IT!
QUAKER BLUEBERRY MUFFIN MIX

Nutrition Facts
Per 1/4 cup (38 g)

Amount	% Daily Value
Calories 160	
Fat 4 g	6%
Saturated 1 g + Trans 0 g	5%
Cholesterol 0 mg	0%
Sodium 300 mg	12%
Carbohydrate 28 g	9%
Fibre 1 g	3%
Sugars 13 g	
Protein 2 g	

20%*

* Based on 1,500 mg per day, the amount recommended by Health Canada for those aged 9–50

blueberry bran muffins

MAKES: 12 MUFFINS

TIME: PREPPING 10 MINUTES, BAKING 15 TO 18 MINUTES

These blueberry bran muffins are tasty, low in salt and a great source of fibre as well, providing 4 g per muffin. I used to make these muffins with baking soda and baking powder both, but the sodium was 160 mg per muffin. By doubling the baking powder and eliminating the baking soda, I reduced the sodium to 87 mg — without impacting the taste of the muffins!

Preheat oven to 375°F (190°C). In a small bowl, combine buttermilk and bran, set aside. In a large bowl, mix together flour and baking powder. In a medium bowl, combine oil, egg, sugar and vanilla. Add bran mixture to sugar mixture and mix. Pour wet ingredients into dry, add blueberries and mix until just combined. Spoon batter into a lightly greased 12-muffin tray, filling cups three-quarters full. Bake for 15 to 18 minutes, until a cake tester inserted into the middle of a muffin comes out clean.

1 CUP (250 ML) BUTTERMILK*
1 CUP (250 ML) NATURAL BRAN
1 CUP (250 ML) WHOLE WHEAT FLOUR
2 TSP (10 ML) BAKING POWDER
¼ CUP (60 ML) VEGETABLE OIL
1 EGG
⅓ CUP (75 ML) BROWN SUGAR
1 TSP (5 ML) VANILLA
¼ CUP (175 ML) BLUEBERRIES (FRESH OR FROZEN)

* TO MAKE BUTTERMILK SUBSTITUTE, COMBINE 1 CUP (250 ML) SKIM MILK WITH 1 TBSP (15 ML) VINEGAR AND LET SIT FOR 5 MINUTES.

MAKE IT!
BLUEBERRY BRAN MUFFINS

Nutrition Facts
Per muffin (54 g)

Amount	% Daily Value
Calories 116	
Fat 5 g	8%
Saturated 1 g + Trans 0 g	3%
Cholesterol 1 mg	0%
Sodium 87 mg	4%
Carbohydrate 17 g	6%
Fibre 4 g	14%
Sugars 6 g	
Protein 3 g	

6%*

* Based on 1,500 mg per day, the amount recommended by Health Canada for those aged 9–50

banana cocoa muffins

MAKES: 16 MUFFINS

TIME: PREPPING 10 MINUTES, BAKING 16 TO 18 MINUTES

3 RIPE BANANAS, MASHED

¼ CUP (60 mL) VEGETABLE OIL

¼ CUP (60 mL) FAT-FREE PLAIN
   YOGOURT OR UNSWEETENED
   APPLESAUCE

2 EGGS

¼ CUP (60 mL) MILK (SKIM OR 1%)

1 TSP (5 mL) VANILLA EXTRACT

1 ¾ CUP (425 mL) WHOLE WHEAT FLOUR

½ CUP (125 mL) SUGAR

2 TBSP (30 mL) COCOA

2 TSP (10 mL) BAKING POWDER

Muffins are a great way to use old bananas because the riper they are, the better the flavour they provide. Bananas for baking can be frozen if you do not plan on using them right away. The cocoa added to this recipe provides a little extra flavour and makes a healthier alternative to chocolate chips. But, best of all, these are low in sodium!

Preheat oven to 375°F (190°C). In a medium bowl, combine bananas, oil, yogourt/applesauce, eggs, milk and vanilla. In a large bowl, combine flour, sugar, cocoa and baking powder. Pour wet ingredients into dry and mix until just combined. Spoon batter into a lightly greased muffin tray, filling cups three-quarters full. Bake for 16 to 18 minutes, until a cake tester inserted into the middle of a muffin comes out clean.

MAKE IT!
BANANA COCOA MUFFINS

Nutrition Facts
Per muffin (58 g)

Amount	% Daily Value
Calories 126	
Fat 4 g	6%
Saturated 0 g + Trans 0 g	2%
Cholesterol 0 mg	0%
Sodium 57 mg	2% 4%*
Carbohydrate 22 g	7%
Fibre 2 g	10%
Sugars 10 g	
Protein 3 g	

* Based on 1,500 mg per day, the amount recommended by Health Canada for those aged 9–50

cranberry orange muffins

MAKES: 12 MUFFINS

TIME: PREPPING 10 MINUTES, BAKING 17 TO 20 MINUTES

Like most berries, cranberries contain antioxidants, which decrease the risk of high blood pressure and heart disease. A good indicator of foods rich in antioxidants is their colour: the darker the fruit or vegetable, the higher the level of antioxidants. The combination of antioxidants, low fat, low salt and high fibre make this a blood-pressure-friendly muffin!

Preheat oven to 400°F (200°C). In a large bowl, combine orange juice, flours, baking powder, rind and cinnamon. In a small bowl, combine sugar, egg, milk and oil. Pour wet ingredients into dry, add cranberries and mix until just combined. Spoon batter into a lightly greased 12-muffin tray. Bake for 17 to 20 minutes, until a cake tester inserted into the middle of a muffin comes out clean.

¼ CUP (60 mL) ORANGE JUICE
1 CUP (250 mL) WHOLE WHEAT FLOUR
¾ CUP (175 mL) ALL-PURPOSE FLOUR
2 TSP (10 mL) BAKING POWDER
1 TBSP (15 mL) ORANGE RIND
1 ½ TSP (7 mL) CINNAMON
⅓ CUP (75 mL) SUGAR
1 EGG, BEATEN
½ CUP (125 mL) MILK (SKIM OR 1%)
¼ CUP (60 mL) VEGETABLE OIL
1 CUP (250 mL) CRANBERRIES, HALVED
   (FRESH OR FROZEN)

MAKE IT!
CRANBERRY ORANGE MUFFINS

Nutrition Facts
Per muffin (48 g)

Amount	% Daily Value
Calories 127	
Fat 5 g	7%
Saturated 0 g + Trans 0 g	2%
Cholesterol 0 mg	0%
Sodium 86 mg	4%
Carbohydrate 19 g	6%
Fibre 2 g	7%
Sugars 7 g	
Protein 3 g	

* Based on 1,500 mg per day, the amount recommended by Health Canada for those aged 9–50

>granola

Granola is something that should be in everyone's pantry. Enjoy it with yogourt, with fruit or by itself, or add just a small handful to a bowl of cereal. It provides a crunch and wholesomeness however you choose to enjoy it.

Often granola is perceived as healthy because it's made with rolled oats, honey, dried fruit, nuts and seeds; unfortunately, this is not usually the case. Although most granolas are not overly high in sodium, they do contain excessive amounts of sugar and saturated fat.

Quaker's Harvest Crunch Honey Nut, for example, contains 50 mg of sodium but 4 g of unhealthy saturated fat and a hefty 14 g of sugar. This is far too high, and unnecessary.

My friend Julie gave me this recipe. This granola is almost sodium-free, low in saturated fat, has less sugar, is higher in potassium than the commercial products and is really tasty. It contains only a quarter of the sugar and saturated fat of the store-bought versions and,

! **although sodium is not overly high in the commercial granolas, it's still 16 times as much as in this homemade recipe.**

Making granola from scratch may require a little more time than purchasing it in a box, but by making your own you can avoid those unhealthy ingredients. Homemade is also much fresher tasting, is cheaper and can be stored in an airtight container for an extended period of time. This goes to show that a little bit of work goes a long way.

HOLD IT!
HARVEST CRUNCH LIGHT & CRISP HONEY NUT CEREAL

Nutrition Facts
Per 1/2 cup (125 mL)

Amount	% Daily Value
Calories 200	
Fat 6 g	9%
Saturated 4 g + Trans 0 g	21%
Cholesterol 0 mg	0%
Sodium 50 mg	2%
Carbohydrate 34 mg	11%
Fibre 2 g	9%
Sugars 14 g	
Protein 4 g	

3%*

* Based on 1,500 mg per day, the amount recommended by Health Canada for those aged 9–50

honey nut granola

MAKES: 5 CUPS (1.2 L)

TIME: PREPPING 10 MINUTES, BAKING 30 TO 35 MINUTES

The focus of this cookbook is on sodium, but in order to get your blood pressure under control you also need to keep your intake of calories and saturated and trans fats in check. I included this recipe because people often inquire about a healthy granola and it is challenging to find one in the stores. This granola is low in sodium and really tasty. It is higher in fat and calories but this is because of nuts and seeds which provide a healthy fat. You can customize it by adding other dried fruit such as cranberries, blueberries, apricots or cherries. You can also add different nuts such as pecans, cashews or walnuts. It is great mixed with yogourt or with berries or cut-up fresh fruit.

Preheat oven to 300°F (150°C). In a large bowl, mix the first 7 ingredients. In a small bowl, mix the remaining ingredients except the apricots. Pour wet mixture into dry, and stir well to mix thoroughly.

Spread the mixture into a baking dish. Bake for 30 to 35 minutes, or until evenly golden brown. Stir every 10 minutes to ensure even browning. Lightly stir again once mixture is out of the oven to keep it from cooling into a solid mass. Mix in apricots. The granola will crisp as it cools. If you use fruit, stir again once it has cooled. Store in the refrigerator in a large freezer bag or other airtight container.

3 CUPS (750 mL) ROLLED OATS
½ CUP (125 mL) UNSALTED SLIVERED ALMONDS
3 TBSP (45 mL) UNSALTED SUNFLOWER SEEDS
1 TBSP (15 mL) SESAME SEEDS
3 TBSP (45 mL) WHEAT GERM
2 TSP (10 mL) CINNAMON
¼ TSP (1 mL) GROUND GINGER
⅓ CUP (75 mL) UNSWEETENED APPLESAUCE
3 TBSP (45 mL) HONEY OR MAPLE SYRUP
2 TBSP (30 mL) CANOLA OIL
½ CUP (125 mL) DRIED APRICOTS, CHOPPED

MAKE IT!
HONEY NUT GRANOLA

Nutrition Facts
Per 1/2 cup (125 mL)

Amount	% Daily Value
Calories 218	
Fat 10 g	15%
Saturated 1 g + Trans 0 g	5%
Cholesterol 0 mg	0%
Sodium 3 mg	0%
Carbohydrate 29 g	10%
Fibre 5 g	18%
Sugars 9 g	
Protein 6 g	

0%*

* Based on 1,500 mg per day, the amount recommended by Health Canada for those aged 9–50

>oatmeal

There is something comforting about a warm bowl of oatmeal to start your day, especially in the colder months before you head outdoors. It also is a filling cereal to tide you over for several hours. It is often enjoyed with a sprinkle of sugar and perhaps some fresh fruit and nuts. For convenience, you can buy handy packages of flavoured instant oatmeal that just require some boiling water. A comfort food certainly doesn't get easier than that.

Sure, most of us know that flavoured instant oatmeal is high in sugar — but, surprisingly, salt has managed to sneak its way in too.

Each of those little packages contains 220 mg of sodium, and the packages are so small that many people will combine two to make one serving.

That's 440 mg of sodium!

To put those numbers into perspective, that is nearly a third of your daily recommended sodium intake, and we don't even think of oatmeal as being particularly salty!

Luckily, cutting the sodium out of your oatmeal is easy! Preparing it is a little more work than just adding boiling water to something from a package, but you'll still have it ready in minutes by using the microwave. You'll reduce that unnecessary salt to 34 mg of sodium and, while you're at it, replace that unnecessary sugar with tastier, nutrient-packed ingredients. This oatmeal will leave you feeling more satisfied for longer than the packaged variety, and you'll never miss that sneaky extra salt.

QUAKER
INSTANT OATMEAL

HIGH FIBRE
4 GRAMS OF FIBRE PER 43 g PACKET

Raisins & Spice

HOLD IT!
QUAKER HIGH FIBRE RAISINS & SPICE OATMEAL

Nutrition Facts
Per 1 packet (43 g)

Amount	% Daily Value
Calories 160	
Fat 1.5 g	2%
Saturated 0.3 g + Trans 0 g	1%
Cholesterol 0 mg	0%
Sodium 220 mg	9%
Carbohydrate 34 g	11%
Fibre 4 g	19%
Sugars 15 g	
Protein 3 g	

15%*

* Based on 1,500 mg per day, the amount recommended by Health Canada for those aged 9–50

cup-a-oatmeal

MAKES: ½ CUP (125 mL)

TIME: LESS THAN 5 MINUTES TOTAL

A nutritious way to start your morning, oatmeal's carbohydrates and fibre give you a boost of prolonged energy. You can even pack this mix up in a freezer bag and take it with you to make in the microwave at work. These oatmeal recipes and the ones that follow are a more generous serving size and still contain far less sodium.

¼ CUP (60 mL) LARGE-FLAKE OATMEAL
½ CUP (125 mL) SKIM MILK OR WATER
¼ CUP (60 mL) LOW-FAT YOGOURT

In a large, deep, microwave-safe bowl or mug, mix oatmeal and milk or water. Cook on high in the microwave for 30 seconds, add yogourt and return to microwave for 1 minute. Give it a stir, and return to microwave for another minute. Remove from microwave, stir and allow to sit for 1 minute.

MAKE IT!
CUP-A-OATMEAL

Nutrition Facts
Per 1/2 cup

Amount	% Daily Value
Calories 103	
Fat 1 g	2%
Saturated 0 g + Trans 0 g	1%
Cholesterol 1 mg	0%
Sodium 34 mg	1%
Carbohydrate 18 g	6%
Fibre 2 g	8%
Sugars 4 g	
Protein 5 g	

2%*

* Based on 1,500 mg per day, the amount recommended by Health Canada for those aged 9–50

high-fibre oatmeal:

For high-fibre oatmeal, stir wheat bran into oatmeal and liquid before cooking. Once oatmeal is cooked and sits for 1 minute, add ground flaxseed.

3 TBSP (45 mL) WHEAT BRAN
1 TBSP (15 mL) GROUND FLAXSEED

MAKE IT!
HIGH-FIBRE OATMEAL

Nutrition Facts
Per 1/2 cup

Amount	% Daily Value
Calories 182	
Fat 6 g	9%
Saturated 0 g + Trans 0 g	2%
Cholesterol 1 mg	0%
Sodium 37 mg	1%
Carbohydrate 28 g	9%
Fibre 10 g	40%
Sugars 4 g	
Protein 8 g	

2%*

* Based on 1,500 mg per day, the amount recommended by Health Canada for those aged 9–50

more oatmeal ideas! 📹

You can easily add extra flavour to your oatmeal without adding extra sodium. Here are some delicious and nutritious suggestions!

blueberry nut oatmeal

Cook oatmeal as directed. If you are using frozen berries, add before cooking and cut water/milk to ⅓ cup (75 mL). If you are using fresh, mix in berries once oatmeal is cooked. Add walnuts once oatmeal is removed from microwave.

¼ CUP (60 mL) BLUEBERRIES (FRESH OR FROZEN)

1 TBSP (15 mL) WALNUT PIECES

apple cinnamon oatmeal

Add raisins before cooking. If you prefer soft apple, add before cooking. For a crispier texture, add apple after cooking. Stir in cinnamon after cooking.

1 TBSP (15 mL) RAISINS (OPTIONAL)

¼ CUP (60 mL) CHOPPED APPLE

CINNAMON, TO TASTE

banana and peanut butter oatmeal

Stir in peanut butter and banana after cooking.

2 TSP (10 mL) PEANUT BUTTER

½ MEDIUM BANANA, CUT INTO CHUNKS

strawberry almond oatmeal

Stir in strawberries and almonds after cooking.

6 STRAWBERRIES, SLICED

1 TBSP (15 mL) UNSALTED SLIVERED ALMONDS

MAKE THEM!
CUP-A-OATMEAL VARIATIONS

Nutrition Facts
Per bowl

blueberry nut oatmeal		banana and peanut butter oatmeal		apple cinnamon oatmeal		strawberry almond oatmeal	
Amount	% Daily Value	Amount	% Daily Value	Amount	% Daily Value	Amount	% Daily Value
Calories 170		Calories 218		Calories 149		Calories 163	
Fat 6 g	9%	Fat 7 g	11%	Fat 2 g	2%	Fat 5 g	7%
Saturated 1 g + Trans 0 g	4%	Saturated 1 g + Trans 0 g	7%	Saturated 0 g + Trans 0 g	2%	Saturated 1 g + Trans 0 g	3%
Cholesterol 1 mg	0%	Cholesterol 1 mg	0%	Cholesterol 1 mg	0%	Cholesterol 1 mg	0%
Sodium 35 mg	2%*	Sodium 86 mg	6%*	Sodium 36 mg	2%*	Sodium 35 mg	2%*
Carbohydrate 25 g	8%	Carbohydrate 34 g	11%	Carbohydrate 30 g	10%	Carbohydrate 25 g	8%
Fibre 3 g Sugars 8 g	14%	Fibre 4 g Sugars 12 g	17%	Fibre 3 g Sugars 14 g	13%	Fibre 4 g Sugars 8 g	17%
Protein 6 g		Protein 8 g		Protein 5 g		Protein 7 g	

* Based on 1,500 mg per day, the amount recommended by Health Canada for those aged 9–50

>pancakes

Pancakes are delicious and a favourite breakfast for many. You can't go wrong with these fluffy cakes dressed up with all your favourite toppings such as butter, maple syrup, fruit and whipped cream. They are so easy to prepare from a dry mix, requiring just a few ingredients and a frying pan. Even easier, you can purchase frozen premade pancakes and just pop them in the toaster. Easy to prepare, yes; but, unfortunately, not without a cost to your health. Commercial pancakes and mixes are loaded with sodium.

! Just ¼ cup (60 mL) of Aunt Jemima batter, enough for 2 pancakes, contains 430 mg of sodium!

Put this into perspective: you want to keep your sodium intake around 1,500 mg a day, and those 2 small pancakes contain 29 per cent of that. That is if you can stop at 2!

Homemade pancakes are just as convenient to prepare as from a mix. All you need to do is add eggs and milk or water to dry ingredients. By preparing them from scratch you are consuming only 165 mg of sodium, which is 61 per cent and 73 per cent less sodium than Aunt Jemima's and Smitty's, respectively. Additional bonus to making them from scratch: you can make any variety you like! The possibilities are endless.

HOLD IT!
AUNT JEMIMA ORIGINAL PANCAKE MIX

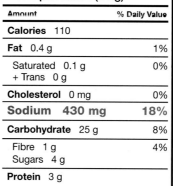

Nutrition Facts
Per 2 pancakes (34 g)

Amount	% Daily Value
Calories 110	
Fat 0.4 g	1%
Saturated 0.1 g + Trans 0 g	0%
Cholesterol 0 mg	0%
Sodium 430 mg	18%
Carbohydrate 25 g	8%
Fibre 1 g	4%
Sugars 4 g	
Protein 3 g	

29%*

* Based on 1,500 mg per day, the amount recommended by Health Canada for those aged 9–50

buttermilk pancakes

MAKES: 14 PANCAKES, 6" (15 CM) DIAMETER

TIME: 15 MINUTES TOTAL

Pancakes are almost a dessert when they're loaded up with sugar and butter. These pancakes, though, provide a healthy breakfast and can be dressed in healthful ways — and still taste like a delicious dessert. With so much potential for flavour and variety, I chose here just my favourite kinds, buttermilk, blueberry and banana and topped them with yogourt and sliced strawberries and bananas. You can add whatever you fancy — chopped apples, raspberries, nuts, cinnamon . . .

In a medium bowl, combine flours, sugar and baking powder. In a small bowl, combine egg, buttermilk and oil. Pour wet ingredients into dry and mix until just combined.

Heat a non-stick skillet (or use oil spray) over medium heat. Add batter — about 2 tbsp (30 mL) per pancake. When batter starts to bubble, flip pancake and continue to cook until browned and cooked through. Serve hot. Top with vanilla yogourt and fruit of your choice or any of the suggestions below.

Top pancakes with your preferred topping:
YOGOURT
SLICED FRUIT OR FRUIT PURÉE
JAM
ICING SUGAR
MAPLE SYRUP (LIMITED AMOUNT)
NUTS

¾ CUP (175 ML) WHOLE WHEAT FLOUR
¾ CUP (175 ML) ALL-PURPOSE FLOUR
2 TBSP (15 ML) SUGAR
2 TSP (10 ML) BAKING POWDER
1 EGG, BEATEN
1 ½ CUPS (375 ML) BUTTERMILK*
1 TBSP (15 ML) CANOLA OIL

* TO MAKE BUTTERMILK SUBSTITUTE, COMBINE 1 ½ CUPS (375 ML) SKIM MILK WITH 1 TBSP (15 ML) VINEGAR AND LET SIT FOR 5 MINUTES.

MAKE IT!
BUTTERMILK PANCAKES

Nutrition Facts
Per 2 pancakes (1/4 cup batter)

Amount	% Daily Value
Calories 157	
Fat 5 g	7%
Saturated 1 g + Trans 0 g	3%
Cholesterol 2 mg	1%
Sodium 165 mg	7%
Carbohydrate 24 g	8%
Fibre 2 g	8%
Sugars 4 g	
Protein 5 g	

11%*

* Based on 1,500 mg per day, the amount recommended by Health Canada for those aged 9–50

delicious pancake twists! 📹

For flavourful new twists on an old favourite, try following the directions on the previous page and then adding the ingredients for either of the two following variations.

blueberry orange pancakes

Add blueberries and orange rind to dry ingredients.

1 CUP (250 mL) BLUEBERRIES (FRESH OR FROZEN)

1 TSP (5 mL) GRATED ORANGE RIND

cinnamon banana pancakes

Add bananas and cinnamon to wet ingredients.

2 RIPE BANANAS, MASHED

½ TSP (2 mL) CINNAMON

MAKE THEM!
BUTTERMILK PANCAKE VARIATIONS

Nutrition Facts
Per 2 pancakes (34 g)

blueberry orange			cinnamon banana		
Amount		% Daily Value	Amount		% Daily Value
Calories 169			Calories 187		
Fat 5 g		8%	Fat 5 g		8%
Saturated 1 g + Trans 0 g		5%	Saturated 1 g + Trans 0 g		5%
Cholesterol 2 mg		1%	Cholesterol 2 mg		1%
Sodium 166 mg		11%*	Sodium 166 mg		11%*
Carbohydrate 27 g		9%	Carbohydrate 32 g		11%
Fibre 2 g Sugars 6 g		8%	Fibre 3 g Sugars 8 g		12%
Protein 6 g			Protein 6 g		

* Based on 1,500 mg per day, the amount recommended by Health Canada for those aged 9–50

>breakfast sandwich

Breakfast is the most important meal of the day. Fast food restaurants and grocery stores now offer endless breakfast options to grab on the run, and breakfast sandwiches are often the food of choice.

These delicious, convenient sandwiches do not make the healthiest of breakfast options, though. Not only are they high in calories and fat and have a low nutritional content, they are very high in salt. McDonald's famous Egg McMuffin contains egg, cheese and ham on an English muffin. It also contains 760 mg of the 1,500 mg recommended sodium.

! **That's half of your sodium for the day, but this sandwich is only a very small part of your daily food consumption.**

If you get the meal and add a hash brown, add an additional 360 mg of sodium.

There is no reason you can't enjoy a delicious breakfast sandwich without causing your daily sodium intake to go through the roof. Compare the Egg McMuffin to the guacamole and cheese breakfast sandwich in our recipe: ours contains fewer calories, less than half the fat and a quarter of the sodium! I will admit that ours will require a little time in the kitchen, but in view of that nutritional comparison, I'd say that time is well spent!

HOLD IT!
McDONALD'S EGG McMUFFIN

Nutrition Facts
Per sandwich

Amount	% Daily Value
Calories 290	
Fat 12 g	18%
Saturated 4.5 g + Trans 0.2 g	24%
Cholesterol 205 mg	68%
Sodium 760 mg	32%
Carbohydrate 29 g	10%
Fibre 2 g Sugars 2 g	8%
Protein 16 g	

51%*

* Based on 1,500 mg per day, the amount recommended by Health Canada for those aged 9–50

cheese and guacamole 📹 breakfast sandwich

MAKES: 2 SERVINGS

TIME: 10 MINUTES TOTAL

Bacon, sausage, cheddar cheese and English muffins all make for sky-high sodium levels in most breakfast sandwiches, so we need alternatives. In this recipe I incorporate more vegetables, limit the bread serving, suggest a lower-sodium cheese, and use avocado as a spread in place of mayo or butter. This is a fresher-tasting, bistro-style sandwich that's far better than the competition. Be sure to check the sodium on the nutritional label for different brands of English muffins, because sodium content can vary from 130 mg to 250 mg per serving. Choose the lowest.

2 TBSP (30 mL) CHOPPED TOMATO

2 TBSP (30 mL) MASHED AVOCADO

A DASH OF GARLIC POWDER

½ TSP (2 mL) LIME JUICE

3 EGG WHITES

¼ TSP (1 mL) DRIED BASIL

2 TBSP (30 mL) CHOPPED GREEN ONION

1 SLICE (1.5 OZ/42 G) LIGHT SWISS CHEESE

1 WHOLE WHEAT ENGLISH MUFFIN, TOASTED

In a small bowl, mix tomato, avocado, garlic powder and lime juice. In another small bowl, mix egg whites, basil and green onion. Pour egg mixture into a non-stick skillet over medium heat. Cook for 1 minute, flip, cut in half, top each half with cheese and continue to cook until bottom side is cooked. Spread avocado mixture over English muffin, top with cooked egg and cheese.

MAKE IT!
CHEESE & GUACAMOLE BREAKFAST SANDWICH

Nutrition Facts

Per sandwich

Amount	% Daily Value
Calories 187	
Fat 5 g	8%
Saturated 3 g + Trans 0 g	15%
Cholesterol 39 mg	13%
Sodium 195 mg	8% 13%*
Carbohydrate 17 g	6%
Fibre 3 g	13%
Sugars 5 g	
Protein 15 g	

* Based on 1,500 mg per day, the amount recommended by Health Canada for those aged 9–50

>quick breads

Nothing beats the flavour or the smell of homemade bread, and even commercial bread has come a long way from the plain whites and whole wheats of a few decades ago.

Whoever would have thought, though, that commercial bread products contain so much unnecessary sodium? Two slices (63 g) of Ben's whole wheat bread have 320 mg — 21 per cent of the daily recommendation for a healthy individual. You want foods that are about 5 per cent per serving, and certainly no more than 10.

! Take into account the filling and the condiments, and the sandwich you thought was a healthy option may be packing more sodium than you realized.

If you have the time, it's best to make homemade bread and omit the salt entirely. Here is a quick bread that is delicious fresh from the oven, or toasted, or warmed and served with soup or beans. It's not at its best in sandwiches, having a rather dense texture, and should be eaten within a day or two, but it takes only about 7 minutes to make, and has only 71 mg of sodium per 45 g slice. You can also incorporate spices, herbs or other components into your bread. I'm suggesting rosemary and garlic in this recipe, but cinnamon, thyme, caraway seed, flaxseed and nuts are all possibilities.

HOLD IT!
BEN'S WHOLE WHEAT BREAD

Nutrition Facts
Per 2 slices (63 g)

Amount	% Daily Value
Calories 150	
Fat 2 g	3%
Saturated 0.5 g + Trans 0 g	3%
Cholesterol 0 mg	0%
Sodium 320 mg	13%
Carbohydrate 28 g	9%
Fibre 3 g	12%
Sugars 3 g	
Protein 6 g	

21%*

* Based on 1,500 mg per day, the amount recommended by Health Canada for those aged 9–50

rosemary and garlic whole wheat bread 📹

MAKES: 16 SLICES

TIME: PREPPING 7 MINUTES, BAKING 45 TO 50 MINUTES

The rosemary and garlic add a subtle flavour, but if you want just plain bread, leave them out. Make sure you don't over-mix the dough. Too much mixing can discourage it from rising. I usually make this bread with all whole wheat flour but some people find that too dense. The flour in this recipe is lightened with some all-purpose, but do feel free to experiment.

Preheat oven to 350ºF (180ºC). In a large bowl, combine first 5 ingredients. In a medium bowl, combine remaining ingredients. Pour wet ingredients into dry and mix until just combined.

Put dough in a loaf pan and bake for 45 to 50 minutes, until a knife inserted in the middle of the loaf comes out clean.

2 CUPS (500 mL) WHOLE WHEAT FLOUR
1 CUP (250 mL) ALL-PURPOSE FLOUR
2 TSP (10 mL) BAKING POWDER
1 TSP (5 mL) DRIED ROSEMARY
1 TSP (5 mL) GARLIC POWDER
1 ½ CUPS (375 mL) BUTTERMILK*
¼ CUP (60 mL) REDUCED-SUGAR MOLASSES
¼ CUP (60 mL) CANOLA OIL

* TO MAKE BUTTERMILK SUBSTITUTE, COMBINE 1 ½ CUPS (375 mL) SKIM MILK WITH 1 TBSP (15 mL) VINEGAR AND LET SIT FOR 5 MINUTES.

MAKE IT!
ROSEMARY AND GARLIC WHOLE WHEAT BREAD

Nutrition Facts
Per 2 slices (90 g)

Amount	% Daily Value
Calories 252	
Fat 8 g	12%
Saturated 0 g + Trans 0 g	0%
Cholesterol 0 mg	0%
Sodium 142 mg	6%
Carbohydrate 40 g	13%
Fibre 6 g	24%
Sugars 6 g	
Protein 8 g	

9%*

* Based on 1,500 mg per day, the amount recommended by Health Canada for those aged 9–50

tortilla bread

MAKES: 10 TORTILLAS

TIME: 20 MINUTES TOTAL

1 CUP (250 ML) WHOLE WHEAT FLOUR
1 CUP (250 ML) ALL-PURPOSE FLOUR
1 TSP (5 ML) BAKING POWDER
¼ CUP (60 ML) CANOLA OIL
½ CUP (250 ML) WARM WATER
COOKING SPRAY

These tortillas are great for fajitas wraps. They will need to be warmed up if you're not using them immediately, though. Just heat them in the microwave for 10 to 15 seconds. Be careful not to overheat them, or they will get really hard.

In a medium bowl, combine flours and baking powder. Add oil and water and mix just until it forms a soft ball. Divide dough into 10 even balls. Place one ball of dough at a time on a floured flat surface. Using a rolling pin, roll out dough until very thin and about 10 in (25 cm) in diameter.

Lightly spray a skillet, and place over medium heat. Once skillet is hot, place flattened dough on skillet and allow to cook for about 30 seconds or until dough starts to bubble. Flip and continue to cook for about 20 to 30 seconds. Repeat for each ball. Cover tortillas with foil and keep warm in oven at 200°F (90°C) for up to 30 minutes. You can refrigerate for up to 3 days or freeze for up to 2 weeks.

MAKE IT!

TORTILLA BREAD

Nutrition Facts
Per tortilla (10 inch diameter)

Amount	% Daily Value
Calories 135	
Fat 6 g	9%
Saturated 0 g + Trans 0 g	2%
Cholesterol 0 mg	0%
Sodium 36 mg	2%
Carbohydrate 18 g	6%
Fibre 2 g Sugars 0 g	7%
Protein 3 g	

2%*

* Based on 1,500 mg per day, the amount recommended by Health Canada for those aged 9–50

Snacks and Appetizers

›wings

Wings make the ideal appetizer and are perfect to pair with a cold beer. Indulging in wings is also easy on the bank account with many bars and restaurants having wing nights when you can buy them at only a few cents each. You can also enjoy wings in the comfort of your own home, with a large selection of frozen wings in a variety of flavours available at the grocery store.

Going out for wing night on occasion or baking up the prepared wings certainly makes a great treat, but if you are doing it often, you may want to reconsider. Wings are super high in fat as most still have the skin, plus they are battered and often deep-fried. The sodium is also a factor.

The commercial brands of wings are convenient, but with convenience comes a cost of about 700 mg of sodium per 4 wings. That is almost half your sodium intake for the day! If you're a wing lover like me, you'll be pleased to know that homemade wings are not only delectable but also contain fewer calories and far less sodium. They contain only 67 mg of sodium per 4 wings. That's one-tenth as much sodium as the commercial kind! Hands down, they are the ultimate choice when it comes to messy wing eating!

! There is a reason why beer pairs so well with wings — to quench your thirst from all that sodium.

HOLD IT!
PC SMOKIN' STAMPEDE WINGS

Nutrition Facts
Per 4 wings (98 g)

Amount	% Daily Value
Calories 220	
Fat 13 g	20%
Saturated 4 g + Trans 0 g	10%
Cholesterol 100 mg	33%
Sodium 670 mg	28%
Carbohydrate 8 g	3%
Fibre 1 g	4%
Sugars 8 g	
Protein 17 g	

45%*

* Based on 1,500 mg per day, the amount recommended by Health Canada for those aged 9–50

President's Choice
le Choix du Président

SMOKIN' STAMPEDE™
chicken wings · cut-up · tips removed · 18% meat protein · fully cooked

STAMPEDE FUMÉ™
ailes de poulet · dépecées · pointes enlevées · 18 % de protéines de viande · cuites à fond

New! Nouveau!
Try it...you'll love it!
Un essai vous convaincra!

907 g | 20 PIECES MINIMUM / MORCEAUX AU MINIMUM | MADE WITH PC® SMOKIN' STAMPEDE™ BEER & CHIPOTLE BARBECUE SAUCE. FAITES AVEC DE LA SAUCE BARBECUE STAMPEDE FUMÉ™ PC® À LA BIÈRE ET AUX PIMENTS CHIPOTLES. | KEEP FROZEN GARDER CONGELÉ

sticky bbq wings

MAKES: 6 SERVINGS (4 WINGS EACH)

TIME: PREPPING 12 MINUTES, COOKING 27 TO 30 MINUTES

This recipe will prove to your guests that wings don't have to have all that extra salt and fat. I recommend removing the skin, in this recipe. It comes off the drumstick part of the wing easily enough, but it can be difficult to remove from the other part. Just trim away and get rid of as much of it as you can. Doing so will significantly cut back on the fat.

12 CHICKEN WINGS

½ CUP (125 mL) BBQ SAUCE (PAGE 82)

Preheat oven to 375°F (190°C). Remove tips of wings and discard. Cut wings in half at the joint and remove and trim away as much of the skin as possible. In a medium bowl, toss wings in BBQ sauce to coat. Spread wings out on a baking sheet. Bake for 15 minutes, turn wings, then bake for additional 12 to 15 minutes until excess sauce is absorbed and wings are slightly browned.

MAKE IT!
STICKY BBQ WINGS

Nutrition Facts
Per 4 wings (97 g)

Amount	% Daily Value
Calories 161	
Fat 8 g	12%
Saturated 2 g + Trans 0 g	8%
Cholesterol 32 mg	11%
Sodium 67 mg	3%
Carbohydrate 13 g	4%
Fibre 1 g	5%
Sugars 9 g	
Protein 10 g	

4%*

* Based on 1,500 mg per day, the amount recommended by Health Canada for those aged 9–50

›hummus

Hummus is a Lebanese dip or spread made from chickpeas, tahini (sesame seed paste), olive oil, garlic and lemon. It's surprising how much flavour comes from such simple ingredients. It's quite versatile and will go with pita bread, crackers or vegetable sticks, and is a healthy alternative to higher-sodium (and higher-fat) condiments such as ketchup and mayo on your sandwich, wrap or burger.

But, be cautious. While not all brands of hummus are overly high in sodium, you do need to consider the serving size on the label compared to how much you would normally eat and the fact that

! the sodium added is unnecessary.

Most hummus contains 115 to 160 mg of sodium per 2 tbsp (30 mL). If you can stick to the 2 tbsp (30 mL) serving, the commercial brands can make a fine choice — but why limit yourself to such a small serving when it comes to this delicious dip?

Fortunately, you can easily enjoy the flavour of hummus and benefit from the fibre and protein it contains, without the excess sodium and fat. Just make it at home. Certainly worth the effort, when you consider that three of these recipes have only 4 mg of sodium per serving: that's 97 per cent less than the commercial brand. Enjoy them guilt-free!

HOLD IT!
SABRA SUPREMELY SPICY HUMMUS

Nutrition Facts
Per 2 tbsp (30 mL)

Amount	% Daily Value
Calories 70	
Fat 6 g	9%
Saturated 0.5 g + Trans 0 g	4%
Cholesterol 0 mg	0%
Sodium 130 mg	5% 9%*
Carbohydrate 4 g	1%
Fibre 1 g	4%
Sugars 0 mg	
Protein 2 g	

* Based on 1,500 mg per day, the amount recommended by Health Canada for those aged 9–50

sun-dried tomato hummus

MAKES: ABOUT 2 CUPS

TIME: 7 MINUTES

I'm suggesting several variations here, and feel free to experiment with such other additions as vegetables, dill, roasted garlic, lime or chili peppers. Starting from dried chickpeas is best; soak them in water overnight and boil them the next day for an hour (or until tender). You can certainly use canned chickpeas if time is short, but check the labels before you buy, bringing home the brand that has the least sodium. And always rinse the brine off canned chickpeas, under running water. It's best to use tahini (sesame paste), but if you don't have that on hand you can use sesame oil instead. Note that the sesame oil does have a stronger sesame flavour.

In a food processor, combine all ingredients and process until smooth. Serve immediately or refrigerate.

2 CUPS (500 mL) CHICKPEAS, PREPARED

½ TBSP (7 mL) OLIVE OIL

½ TBSP (7 mL) TAHINI PASTE

2 CLOVES GARLIC, CHOPPED

¼ TSP (1 mL) CUMIN

2 TBSP (30 mL) LIGHT SOUR CREAM

2 TBSP (30 mL) LOW-FAT PLAIN
  YOGOURT

PINCH OF CAYENNE

JUICE FROM 1 MEDIUM LEMON

3 TBSP (45 mL) SUN-DRIED TOMATOES

PEPPER TO TASTE

MAKE IT!

SUN-DRIED TOMATO HUMMUS

Nutrition Facts
Per 2 tbsp (30 mL)

Amount	% Daily Value
Calories 46	
Fat 2 g	2%
Saturated 0 g + Trans 0 g	2%
Cholesterol 17 mg	6%
Sodium 4 mg	<1%
Carbohydrate 7 g	2%
Fibre 2 g	7%
Sugars 1 g	
Protein 2 g	

1%*

* Based on 1,500 mg per day, the amount recommended by Health Canada for those aged 9–50

more hummus flavours!

To add a little variety to your hummus without adding salt, try following the directions on the previous page and then adding any of these additional ingredients.

spicy hummus

1 TSP (15 ML) DRIED CHILI PEPPER FLAKES

jalapeño hummus

1 JALAPEÑO, SEEDED AND CHOPPED

roasted red pepper hummus

1 ROASTED RED PEPPER*, CHOPPED

* TO ROAST PEPPERS, CUT IN HALVES, REMOVE SEEDS AND PLACE PEPPERS OPEN SIDE DOWN ON A BAKING SHEET. BROIL UNTIL SKINS ARE BLACKENED. ONCE COOLED, REMOVE AND DISCARD SKIN, THEN CHOP THE PEPPERS. ONE ROASTED RED PEPPER YIELDS ABOUT $\frac{1}{4}$ CUP (60 ML) CHOPPED. YOU CAN PURCHASE BOTTLED ROASTED RED PEPPERS IN A PINCH BUT KEEP IN MIND THAT THEY DO CONTAIN ADDED SALT; IT'S BEST TO ROAST YOUR OWN. ROASTED, SKINNED PEPPERS ALSO FREEZE WELL.

MAKE THEM!
HUMMUS VARIATIONS

Nutrition Facts
Per 2 tbsp (30 mL)

spicy hummus		jalapeño hummus		roasted red pepper hummus	
Amount	**% Daily Value**	**Amount**	**% Daily Value**	**Amount**	**% Daily Value**
Calories 44		**Calories** 46		**Calories** 47	
Fat 1 g	2%	**Fat** 2 g	2%	**Fat** 2 g	2%
Saturated 0 g + Trans 0 g	2%	Saturated 0 g + Trans 0 g	2%	Saturated 0 g + Trans 0 g	2%
Cholesterol 1 mg	0%	**Cholesterol** 1 mg	0%	**Cholesterol** 1 mg	0%
Sodium 4 mg	<1%*	Sodium 4 mg	<1%*	Sodium 4 mg	<1%*
Carbohydrate 6 g	2%	**Carbohydrate** 6 g	2%	**Carbohydrate** 7 g	2%
Fibre 2 g Sugars 1 g	6%	Fibre 2 g Sugars 1 g	7%	Fibre 2 g Sugars 1 g	7%
Protein 2 g		**Protein** 2 g		**Protein** 2 g	

* Based on 1,500 mg per day, the amount recommended by Health Canada for those aged 9–50

›chips

If you tend to crave saltier snack foods, chips are likely at the top of your list. The satisfying crunch and the variety of flavours make chips so desirable. And we're no longer limited to just potato chips; veggie chips, tortilla chips, pita chips — all provide that crunch that you look for in a chip.

I'm not one to bash chips, because I haven't come across one person who dislikes them. The reality is, though, that they should definitely not be on your list of commonly eaten foods.

And don't be fooled about the baked varieties: they still contain high levels of sodium and calories, even though some may be low in fat. Keep in mind that the daily sodium recommendation is 1,500 mg a day and it's important not to surpass 2,300 mg a day.

Flavoured baked chips contain 360 mg of sodium per 50 g!

That's a lot of sodium in one small bag of chips. The original, unflavoured baked chips have less sodium, but 310 mg is still too much.

Can't stop after eating just one? Now you won't have to limit yourself. These pita chips take only minutes to bake and they taste great, either with various seasonings or plain. The nutritional facts are great as well, with only 171 mg of sodium per serving. Perhaps next time you're standing in line at the checkout, you'll think twice about buying that bag of chips.

HOLD IT!
OLD DUTCH BAKED CREAMY DILL CHIPS

Nutrition Facts
Per 30 chips (50 g)

Amount	% Daily Value
Calories 210	
Fat 4 g	6%
Saturated 0.5 g + Trans 0 g	3%
Cholesterol 0 mg	0%
Sodium 360 mg	15%
Carbohydrate 40 g	13%
Fibre 2 g	8%
Sugars 5 g	
Protein 4 g	

24%*

* Based on 1,500 mg per day, the amount recommended by Health Canada for those aged 9–50

crunchy plain pita chips

MAKES: 3 SERVINGS (1 PITA EACH)

TIME: PREPPING 8 MINUTES, COOKING 6 TO 8 MINUTES

These are so quick to prepare, and they provide the satisfying crunch of a potato chip without all that salt and fat. Season them however you like, either to complement a dip or to enjoy alone — all the variations below taste good to me. And consider buying a manual oil sprayer and filling it at home. That's both cheaper and more environmentally friendly than using the canned, branded oil sprays. If you don't have an oil sprayer, just use a light touch with a brush.

Preheat oven to 350°F (180°C). Lay pitas out flat, with the inside facing up. Spray with oil for 2 seconds per pita half. Cut pita like a pizza to make 12 triangular wedges. Place on a baking sheet in a single layer. Bake for 6 to 8 minutes until slightly browned and crisp. Watch carefully; they burn very easily.

3 WHOLE WHEAT PITAS, SPLIT HORIZONTALLY TO GIVE 6 CIRCULAR HALVES

OIL SPRAY

MAKE IT!
CRUNCHY PLAIN PITA CHIPS

Nutrition Facts
Per pita (50 g)

Amount	% Daily Value
Calories 158	
Fat 1.5 g	2%
Saturated 0 g + Trans 0 g	0%
Cholesterol 0 mg	0%
Sodium 171 mg	7% 11%*
Carbohydrate 29 g	10%
Fibre 2 g	8%
Sugars 1 g	
Protein 6 g	

* Based on 1,500 mg per day, the amount recommended by Health Canada for those aged 9–50

seasoned pita chips

Follow directions on previous page but mix seasonings in a bowl, then sprinkle them evenly over the pitas before spraying with oil.

herb and garlic pita chips

1 ½ TSP (7 mL) GARLIC POWDER
1 ½ TSP (7 mL) ITALIAN SEASONING

rosemary and parmesan pita chips

1 ½ TSP (7 mL) DRIED ROSEMARY
2 TBSP (30 mL) PARMESAN CHEESE, GRATED
1 TSP (5 mL) PAPRIKA

sweet chili pita chips

2 TSP (10 mL) DRIED CHILI PEPPER FLAKES
2 TSP (10 mL) BROWN SUGAR

spicy onion and thyme pita chips

¼ TO ½ TSP (1 TO 2 mL) CAYENNE (DEPENDING ON HOW SPICY YOU WANT IT)
1 ½ TSP (7 mL) DRIED THYME
1 TBSP (15 mL) ONION POWDER

MAKE THEM!

SEASONED PITA CHIPS

Nutrition Facts
Per pita (50 g)

herb and garlic pita chips		sweet chili pita chips		rosemary and parmesan pita chips		spicy onion and thyme pita chips	
Amount	**% Daily Value**	**Amount**	**% Daily Value**	**Amount%**	**% Daily Value**	**Amount**	**% Daily Value**
Calories 158		**Calories** 169		**Calories** 172		**Calories** 158	
Fat 1.5 g	2%	**Fat** 1.5 g	2%	**Fat** 2.5 g	4%	**Fat** 1.5 g	2%
Saturated 0 g + Trans 0 g	0%	Saturated 0 g + Trans 0 g	0%	Saturated 1 g + Trans 0 g	5%	Saturated 0 g + Trans 0 g	0%
Cholesterol 0 mg	0%	**Cholesterol** 0 mg	0%	**Cholesterol** 3 mg	1%	**Cholesterol** 0 mg	0%
Sodium 171 mg	11%*	Sodium 171 mg	11%*	Sodium 222 mg	15%*	Sodium 171 mg	11%*
Carbohydrate 29 g	10%	**Carbohydrate** 32 g	11%	**Carbohydrate** 29 g	10%	**Carbohydrate** 29 g	10%
Fibre 2 g Sugars 1 g	8%	Fibre 2 g Sugars 4 g	8%	Fibre 2 g Sugars 1 g	8%	Fibre 2 g Sugars 1 g	8%
Protein 6 g		**Protein** 6 g		**Protein** 7 g		**Protein** 6 g	

* Based on 1,500 mg per day, the amount recommended by Health Canada for those aged 9–50

›crackers

Crackers can be a nutritious and convenient snack, and a great companion for cheese, hors d'oeuvres or soups. They can also cause you to exceed your daily recommended sodium without noticing. Crackers may seem to be fairly low in sodium, according to the nutritional information on the package, but only because the serving sizes are typically so small (usually 2 crackers). Even at that, sodium content per serving can range from 50 to 275 mg. While flavourings may include herbs or seeds, that sodium comes from salt often added to the dough or sprinkled on top (or both!) before baking. Stoned wheat thins may seem healthy at first glance since they have no cholesterol or trans fat, but just 3 of these crackers contain 240 mg of sodium! This is 16 per cent of your daily recommended limit of sodium, from one small snack (which you may be eating with cheese, soups or other foods that also contain sodium).

Certain varieties of crackers are produced in reduced-sodium versions, and some kinds of crackers (such as saltines) are more heavily salted, so choose carefully. Or better yet, use the following recipe. It offers a delicious way to avoid sodium while still getting gourmet taste. Even with a larger, more realistic serving size, the sodium is much lower than the commercial product.

HOLD IT!
STONED WHEAT THINS

Nutrition Facts
Per 3 crackers (21 g)

Amount	% Daily Value
Calories 90	
Fat 2 g	3%
Saturated 0.4 g + Trans 0 g	2%
Cholesterol 0 mg	0%
Sodium 240 mg	10%
Carbohydrate 15 g	5%
Fibre 1 g Sugars 0 g	4%
Protein 2 g	

16%*

* Based on 1,500 mg per day, the amount recommended by Health Canada for those aged 9–50

almond cranberry crisps

MAKES: APPROX. 100 CRACKERS

TIME: PREPPING 15 MINUTES, COOKING 60 TO 75 MINUTES

These chewy, delicious crackers are inspired by an artisanal brand available at specialty shops, and pair well with goat cheese or brie. You can experiment with different fruits or nuts. Try slicing and baking one loaf and popping the other, unsliced, into the freezer for later; it is a great thing to have on hand.

Preheat oven to 350°F (180°C). In a large bowl, stir together flours, baking powder and cinnamon. Add buttermilk, oil, brown sugar and honey and stir a few strokes. Toss cranberries in a small amount of flour. Add the cranberries, almonds and flaxseed and stir just until blended.

Pour the batter into 2 loaf pans (4 x 8 inch/10 x 20 cm) that have been sprayed with non-stick spray. Bake for about 35 to 45 minutes until golden and springy to the touch. Remove from the pans and cool on a wire rack.

The cooler the bread, the easier it is to slice really thin. You can leave it until the next day or place it in the freezer. Slice the loaves as thin as you can and place the slices in a single layer on an ungreased cookie sheet. Preheat the oven to 300°F (150°C) and bake them for about 15 minutes, then flip them over and bake for another 10 minutes, until crisp and deep golden.

1 CUP ALL-PURPOSE FLOUR
1 CUP WHOLE WHEAT FLOUR
2 TSP BAKING POWDER
2 TSP (10 ML) CINNAMON
2 CUPS (500 ML) BUTTERMILK*
¼ CUP (60 ML) CANOLA OIL
2 TBSP (30 ML) BROWN SUGAR
3 TBSP (30 ML) HONEY
¼ CUP (60 ML) DRIED CRANBERRIES
2 TBSP (30 ML) SLIVERED ALMONDS
3 TBSP (45 ML) GROUND FLAXSEED
COOKING SPRAY

* TO MAKE BUTTERMILK SUBSTITUTE, COMBINE 2 CUPS (500 ML) SKIM MILK WITH 2 TBSP (30 ML) VINEGAR AND LET SIT FOR 5 MINUTES.

MAKE IT!
ALMOND CRANBERRY CRISPS

Nutrition Facts
Per 5 crackers (40 g)

Amount	% Daily Value
Calories 101	
Fat 3 g	5%
Saturated 0 g + Trans 0 g	2%
Cholesterol 1 mg	0%
Sodium 62 mg	3%
Carbohydrate 17 g	5%
Fibre 1 g	4%
Sugars 6 g	
Protein 2 g	

4%*

* Based on 1,500 mg per day, the amount recommended by Health Canada for those aged 9–50

›snack mix

I love buffet and pot-luck eating, where you get to taste a combination of dishes. Snack mixes must be the buffets of snack foods, with different tastes and textures in every crunchy bite. From Bits & Bites to Party Mix to Munchies Snack Mix, I love them all. The only issue seems to be to decide which brand you like best.

But if this is something you regularly indulge in, it may be time to re-evaluate. The baked versions may sound healthier, but even baking doesn't affect how much oil or salt is added before cooking. Commercial snack mixes are high in sodium, calories and fat. The nutritional information on the package says it all.

! An 85-g bag of Humpty Dumpty Party Mix contains 810 mg of sodium!

What does this mean? You're getting 54 per cent of your recommended sodium in just this snack food. The serving size is also far too large and high in calories.

Happily, here is an alternative to these high-salt, high-fat commercial mixes. The recipe that follows is a healthier option that tastes great and has the crunch of the commercial mixes, but with less than half the sodium per serving, at only 238 mg per cup. The serving size is smaller than the store-bought mix, but the sodium content is still way lower, proportionately.

HOLD IT!
HUMPTY DUMPTY PARTY MIX

Nutrition Facts
Per bag (85 g)

Amount	% Daily Value
Calories 420	
Fat 22 g	34%
Saturated 3 g + Trans 3 g	30%
Cholesterol 0 mg	0%
Sodium 810 mg	**34%**
Carbohydrate 52 g	17%
Fibre 2 g	8%
Sugars 3 g	
Protein 5 g	

54%*

* Based on 1,500 mg per day, the amount recommended by Health Canada for those aged 9–50

party mix

MAKES: 4 CUPS (1 L)

TIME: ABOUT 10 MINUTES TOTAL

This party mix has less sodium and less fat, but still provides that satisfying crunch that you look for in a snack food. The recipe calls for peanuts, but you can substitute cashews, pecans or almonds, or omit the nuts entirely. I use broken-up rice cakes here, but you could use plain popcorn. The cereals in this recipe are just suggestions. You can use whichever variety you prefer, such as oat squares, corn flakes, etc.

In a large microwave-safe bowl, combine cereals, pretzels, rice cakes and peanuts. In a small bowl, mix melted margarine or butter, Worcestershire sauce, onion powder, garlic powder and chili powder. Pour half of spice mixture over cereal mixture and mix. Pour remaining spice mixture over cereal mixture and mix again to coat. Microwave on high for 2 minutes. Toss mixture and microwave for 1 minute more. Toss again and microwave for an additional minute. Sauce should be absorbed and mix should be crisp. Allow to cool. Once cool, serve immediately or place in an airtight container.

¾ CUP (175 ML) WOVEN WHOLE WHEAT SQUARES (E.G., SHREDDIES)

¾ CUP (175 ML) CORN BRAN CEREAL

¾ CUP (175 ML) DOUGHNUT-SHAPED OAT CEREAL (E.G., CHEERIOS)

1 CUP (250 ML) UNSALTED PRETZELS

2 PLAIN RICE CAKES, EACH BROKEN INTO ABOUT 25 PIECES

¼ CUP (60 ML) UNSALTED PEANUTS (OPTIONAL)

1 TBSP (15 ML) NON-HYDROGENATED UNSALTED MARGARINE OR UNSALTED BUTTER, MELTED

4 TSP (20 ML) WORCESTERSHIRE SAUCE

2 TSP (10 ML) ONION POWDER

1 TSP (5 ML) GARLIC POWDER

2 TSP (10 ML) CHILI POWDER

MAKE IT!

PARTY MIX

Nutrition Facts	
Per 1 cup (50 g)	
Amount	**% Daily Value**
Calories 163	
Fat 4 g	6%
Saturated 1 g	4%
+ Trans 0 g	
Cholesterol 0 mg	0%
Sodium 238 mg	10%
Carbohydrate 30 g	10%
Fibre 3 g	12%
Sugars 5 g	
Protein 3 g	

16%*

* Based on 1,500 mg per day, the amount recommended by Health Canada for those aged 9–50

>salsa

Salsa has gone mainstream. You don't find it only with nachos now, but taking the place of popular condiments such as ketchup and mustard. It's a great way to dress up eggs, chicken, fish, hamburgers, sandwiches and many other foods. Salsa can be a healthy choice, too, offering vegetables but little or no fat.

Unfortunately, though, many commercial salsas contain a lot of added sodium. Old El Paso brand's nutritional information reveals an alarming 440 mg per scant 1/4 cup (60 mL). That's 29 per cent of your recommended daily amount. And that salsa will be only a small part of the meal when you're using it as a dip or a condiment. Adding commercial salsa to food that is already high in sodium, like nachos or fajitas, can put the sodium content of your meal through the roof.

Fortunately, the herbs and spices in salsa make it easy to omit the salt. In this recipe, cilantro, garlic and lemon juice provide the high notes for a flavoursome salsa that you can easily make at home, and the salsa is not only healthier than commercial brands but quick to prepare and much fresher tasting. Best of all, it has only 6 mg of sodium per 1/4 cup (60 mL). **That's 434 mg less than the amount stated in that commercial product's nutritional information.** Once you've tasted homemade salsa you'll never go back to store-bought.

HOLD IT!
OLD EL PASO THICK N' CHUNKY SALSA

Nutrition Facts
Per 1/4 cup (60 mL)

Amount	% Daily Value
Calories 25	
Fat 0 g	0%
Saturated 0 g + Trans 0 g	0%
Cholesterol 0 mg	0%
Sodium 440 mg	18%
Carbohydrate 5 g	2%
Fibre 1 g Sugars	4%
Protein 0 g	

29%*

* Based on 1,500 mg per day, the amount recommended by Health Canada for those aged 9–50

salsa

MAKES: 2 CUPS (500 ML)

TIME: ABOUT 10 MINUTES

This recipe calls for no-added-salt diced tomatoes, which you can find at many grocery stores. If you can't find them, though, either use diced fresh tomatoes (approximately 2 cups/500 mL) or read some labels and choose the lowest-sodium canned tomatoes you can find.

In a food processor, process garlic, onion, jalapeño and lime juice for 30 seconds to a minute until minced. Add canned and fresh tomatoes, green pepper and cilantro, and process until it's the consistency you like — shorter for chunky, longer for fine. Add pepper to taste.

variations:

For a spicy salsa, leave in some or all of the seeds from the jalapeño.

Add any or all of the following:

1 CUP (250 ML) FROZEN CORN KERNELS, THAWED

HALF AN AVOCADO, DICED

1 CUP (250 ML) BLACK BEANS

1 CLOVE GARLIC, CHOPPED

¼ CUP (60 ML) CHOPPED ONION

1 JALAPEÑO, SEEDED*, MINCED

JUICE FROM 1 LIME, OR 1 TBSP (15 ML) LIME JUICE

1 CAN (28 FL OZ/796 ML) NO-ADDED-SALT DICED TOMATOES, DRAINED

1 MEDIUM FRESH TOMATO, DICED (OPTIONAL)

1 GREEN PEPPER, CHOPPED

1 TBSP (15 ML) CILANTRO, MINCED

PEPPER TO TASTE

* IF YOU LIKE HOT SALSA, INCLUDE SEEDS BUT KEEP IN MIND THEY CONTAIN A LOT OF HEAT.

MAKE IT!

SALSA

Nutrition Facts
Per ¼ cup (60 mL)

Amount	% Daily Value
Calories 14	
Fat 0 g	0%
Saturated 0 g + Trans 0 g	0%
Cholesterol 0 mg	0%
Sodium 6 mg	0%
Carbohydrate 3 g	1%
Fibre 1 g	4%
Sugars 2 g	
Protein 1 g	

0%*

* Based on 1,500 mg per day, the amount recommended by Health Canada for those aged 9–50

>bruschetta

Bruschetta is an Italian appetizer made with tomatoes, onion, olive oil, cheese, balsamic vinegar and basil. The mixture of vegetables provides a very fresh taste and aroma and, conveniently enough, you can purchase bruschetta ready-made. No longer considered just an appetizer, this tomato mixture can be enjoyed as the sauce on a pizza, or on chicken, fish or in a wrap.

Bruschetta is high in potassium from the tomatoes. Potassium-rich foods can counteract the effects of sodium, and that's good, because commercial bruschetta preparations contain unnecessary salt.

! **Commercial bruschetta contains 170 mg of sodium per 2 tbsp (30 mL) serving.**

There are certainly far worse appetizers out there but that extra salt just isn't needed. Besides, what is the actual serving size you usually consume? Likely more than 2 tbsp.

Tomatoes, balsamic vinegar, garlic and basil provide all the flavour you need. You can make a healthy and tasty bruschetta in only 10 minutes. The commercial products include an unnecessary amount of cheese, adding even more sodium (and fat), while this recipe calls for just enough cheese to provide flavour without overdoing the sodium. Here, we have only 4 mg of sodium per 2 tbsp (30 mL). That is 42 times less sodium than the commercial kind and you have to invest only a few additional minutes to prepare it.

KEEP REFRIGERATED/GARDER AU FROID
227 g/8 oz

HOLD IT!

SUMMER FRESH BRUSCHETTA

Nutrition Facts
Per 2 tbsp (30 mL)

Amount	% Daily Value
Calories 30	
Fat 2.5 g	4%
Saturated 0 g + Trans 0 g	0%
Cholesterol 0 mg	0%
Sodium 170 mg	7%
Carbohydrate 2 g	1%
Fibre 0 g Sugars 1 g	0%
Protein 0.3 g	

11%*

* Based on 1,500 mg per day, the amount recommended by Health Canada for those aged 9–50

garlic bruschetta

MAKES: 1 LOAF

TIME: PREPPING 5 MINUTES, COOKING 12 TO 16 MINUTES

Delicious on a toasted baguette, bruschetta can also be used as a pizza sauce, in a wrap, on a burger or a fajita, with fish or with nachos. If you can't find no-added-salt canned diced tomatoes, just use diced fresh tomatoes instead.

Preheat oven to 400°F (200°C). Place sliced bread on a baking sheet and toast for 6 to 8 minutes. In a medium bowl, combine remaining ingredients except whole cloves of garlic. Once bread is removed from the oven, rub one side of each piece with peeled clove of garlic. Spoon bruschetta mixture on slices of bread. Bake for 6 to 8 minutes, until bottoms are toasted.

variations:

Instead of the Monterey Jack, use grated Swiss, crumbled goat cheese or grated mozzarella.

1 WHOLE WHEAT BAGUETTE, SLICED INTO 1-INCH (2.5-CM) ROUNDS

1 CAN (28 FL OZ/796 ML) NO-ADDED-SALT DICED TOMATOES

¼ CUP (60 ML) DICED RED ONION

2 CLOVES GARLIC, MINCED

1 TBSP (15 ML) BALSAMIC VINEGAR

½ TSP (2 ML) DRIED BASIL

½ TBSP (7 ML) OLIVE OIL

3 TBSP (45 ML) GRATED LIGHT MONTEREY JACK

PEPPER TO TASTE

2 CLOVES GARLIC, WHOLE, PEELED

MAKE IT!

GARLIC BRUSCHETTA

Nutrition Facts
Per 2 tbsp (30 mL)

Amount	% Daily Value
Calories 13	
Fat 1 g	1%
Saturated 0 g + Trans 0 g	1%
Cholesterol 0 mg	0%
Sodium 4 mg	0%
Carbohydrate 2 g	1%
Fibre 0 g	1%
Sugars 1 g	
Protein 0 g	

0%*

* Based on 1,500 mg per day, the amount recommended by Health Canada for those aged 9–50

›chip and veggie dips

I'm not a potato chip hater, but I'm not a huge fan of plain chips, either — unless they're paired with a good dip. It's the same with vegetables. I could eat trays of veggies — if they're accompanied by a good dip. My friend Meghan reminded me just how much we North Americans love our dips and condiments. After nearly two years in Brazil, where dips are not used, she became acutely aware that French fries, raw vegetables and potato chips are, well, bare without dips.

Most commercial dips, though, are based on mayo or sour cream, which makes them high in both sodium and fat. Loading vegetables with these dips lessens the healthy boost you'd otherwise get. Dip your chips in these, and you're pairing fat with fat and piling salt on salt.

A 2-tbsp (30-mL) serving of Ruffles French Onion Dip contains 230 mg of sodium. If you're trying to stay within the recommended 1,500 mg of sodium per day, 230 mg presents a problem; and it's only in a condiment!

For that matter, you probably won't stop at only 2 tbsp (30 mL) of dip.

Not to worry, to that problem I have the solution. Homemade dip does require a little more work than just purchasing the prepared varieties, but your health should be worth the small sacrifice. The salmon dill dip on the following page not only tastes great but is also much more nutritious than the commercial type. The salmon is a source of heart-healthy omega-3 fatty acids, and has both less fat and much less sodium. In fact, by choosing this dip instead of the commercial kind, you are saving 174 mg of sodium per 2 tbsp (30 mL)! Better yet, if you're craving a dip with a bite, try the chipotle and roasted red pepper dip with only 14 mg of sodium per 2 tbsp (30 mL). Go ahead, get dipping!

HOLD IT!
RUFFLES ONION DIP

Nutrition Facts
Per 2 tbsp (30 mL)

Amount	% Daily Value
Calories 60	
Fat 5 g	7%
Saturated 0.5 g + Trans 0 g	2%
Cholesterol 5 mg	1%
Sodium 230 mg	10%
Carbohydrate 2 g	1%
Fibre 0 g	0%
Sugars 0 g	
Protein 1 g	

15%*

* Based on 1,500 mg per day, the amount recommended by Health Canada for those aged 9–50

salmon dill dip

MAKES: 1 CUP (250 ML)

TIME: ABOUT 10 MINUTES TOTAL

Low in sodium (and fat), this is a great dip to have with crackers, pita chips or vegetable sticks, or to spread on a baguette or a bagel. Canned salmon includes bones and skin. I recommend removing the skin but the bones are a good source of calcium, so mash them in with the fish. If you can't find lower-sodium canned salmon where you shop, just use 3/4 cup (175 mL) of salmon that you've cooked yourself.

In a medium bowl, combine salmon, yogourt, cream cheese, horseradish and dill. Heat butter in a non-stick frying pan over high heat. Sauté onion until browned, 2 to 3 minutes. Mix onion into dip. Add pepper to taste. Serve immediately, or refrigerate for several hours for maximum flavour.

1 CAN (213 G) NO-ADDED-SALT SALMON, DRAINED AND MASHED

½ CUP (125 ML) LOW-FAT PLAIN YOGOURT

2 TBSP (30 ML) LIGHT PLAIN CREAM CHEESE, SOFTENED

1 ½ TSP (7 ML) HORSERADISH

1 TBSP (15 ML) MINCED FRESH DILL

½ TSP (2 ML) BUTTER OR MARGARINE

2 GREEN ONIONS, CHOPPED

PEPPER TO TASTE

MAKE IT!
SALMON DILL DIP

Nutrition Facts
Per 2 tbsp (30 mL)

Amount	% Daily Value
Calories 59	
Fat 3 g	4%
Saturated 1 g + Trans 0 g	4%
Cholesterol 18 mg	6%
Sodium 56 mg	2%
Carbohydrate 2 g	1%
Fibre 0 g	1%
Sugars 2 g	
Protein 7 g	

4%*

* Based on 1,500 mg per day, the amount recommended by Health Canada for those aged 9–50

chipotle and roasted red pepper dip

MAKES: 1 CUP (250 ML)

TIME: 10 MINUTES

Not limited only to dipping, this can be used as a spread on bread, in a sandwich or on a burger. The chipotle gives it a great mesquite taste with a little bite and the lime lends a complementary citrus zip. Sour cream makes a great base for dips but it also contains sodium, so I replaced some of it with plain yogourt. Not to worry, though, this dip is still bursting with flavour. You can serve it right away but it's best to refrigerate it for several hours to allow the flavours to be at their maximum.

In a small bowl, combine all ingredients.

⅓ CUP (75 ML) LIGHT SOUR CREAM

¼ CUP (60 ML) LOW-FAT PLAIN YOGOURT

1 LARGE ROASTED RED PEPPER*, CHOPPED

2 GREEN ONIONS, CHOPPED

1 TSP (5 ML) DRIED CHIPOTLE

JUICE FROM HALF A LIME

RIND FROM HALF A LIME, MINCED

* FOR ROASTING DIRECTIONS, SEE PAGE 40.

MAKE IT!
CHIPOTLE AND ROASTED RED PEPPER DIP

Nutrition Facts
Per 2 tbsp (30 mL)

Amount	% Daily Value
Calories 27	
Fat 1 g	2%
Saturated 1 g + Trans 0 g	4%
Cholesterol 4 mg	1%
Sodium 14 mg	1%
Carbohydrate 3 g	1%
Fibre 1 g	2%
Sugars 2 g	
Protein 1 g	

1%*

* Based on 1,500 mg per day, the amount recommended by Health Canada for those aged 9–50

Soups, Salads and Side Dishes

›fish and seafood chowder

Seafood and fish chowder is definitely one of those comfort foods with its creamy texture and abundance of fish/seafood and vegetables. It's rich in nutrients. The fish and seafood provide a great source of the heart-healthy omega-3 fatty acids. The milk and vegetables in a chowder also provide lots of vitamins and minerals. Paired with a roll or biscuit, it's a well-rounded meal in a bowl.

I'm a big fan of seafood chowder, but canned chowder just doesn't have that fresh delicious flavour. In addition,

! the sodium in the canned version is far too high.

Campbell's Healthy Request New England Clam Chowder bears the Heart Check logo but it still contains 480 mg per cup, which is more than twice the sodium that any food serving should have if your blood pressure is high or you are at risk. It is better than regular Campbell's New England Clam Chowder, though.

! That has 870 mg!

Even homemade chowder can be a problem, since the broth or stock used, and especially any smoked or salted fish, can quickly jack up the sodium and fat to unacceptable levels.

With the help of my good friend chef Craig Flinn, I came up with a great-tasting chowder that has only 248 mg of sodium per cup. This chowder contains more seafood than the canned variety and, of course, tastes much fresher. You can also freeze it, to have when you want it. You don't have to settle for chowder from a can.

HOLD IT!
CAMPBELL'S NEW ENGLAND CLAM CHOWDER

Nutrition Facts
Per 1 cup (250 mL)

Amount	% Daily Value
Calories 200	
Fat 13 g	21%
Saturated 2.5 g + Trans 0.1 g	12%
Cholesterol 5 mg	1%
Sodium 870 mg	36%
Carbohydrate 16 g	5%
Fibre 4 g	14%
Sugars 1 g	
Protein 4 g	

58% *

* Based on 1,500 mg per day, the amount recommended by Health Canada for those aged 9–50

creamy seafood chowder

MAKES: 4 SERVINGS

TIME: 20 MINUTES TOTAL

The herbs and other ingredients spice up this recipe. I use a commercial frozen seafood mix here that contains scallops, shrimp, salmon and mixed white fish, but you could also use lobster or crab or just about any fish you want. Although the calories may be higher in the homemade version, that's because it's packed with more stuff. This chowder is going to keep your hunger satisfied longer and provide more protein, heart-healthy fat, vitamins and minerals.

In a non-stick saucepan over medium heat, melt margarine and add onion and garlic. Sauté for 1 to 2 minutes, until onion is browned. Add celery, carrot and potatoes and sauté until potato is slightly tender, about 6 to 8 minutes. Mix in cornstarch/water mixture and celery seed. Add broth and wine. Bring to a boil, stirring occasionally, and cover. Continue stirring occasionally, and cook until potato is tender. Reduce heat to low, add chowder mix and continue to cook for about 5 minutes or until fish is opaque. Stir in milk and tarragon and heat just to serving temperature; do not let boil.

1 TBSP (15 mL) NON-HYDROGENATED MARGARINE

1 SMALL ONION, CHOPPED

1 CLOVE GARLIC, MINCED OR FINELY CHOPPED

1 STALK CELERY, CHOPPED

1 MEDIUM CARROT, PEELED AND CHOPPED

2 MEDIUM POTATOES, PEELED AND CHOPPED INTO SMALL PIECES

2 TBSP (30 mL) CORNSTARCH MIXED WITH EQUAL AMOUNT WATER

½ TSP (2 mL) CELERY SEED

1 CUP (250 mL) LOW-SODIUM CHICKEN BROTH

½ CUP (125 mL) WHITE WINE

¾ LB (340 G) CHOWDER MIX

1 CAN (12 FL OZ/370 mL) NON-FAT EVAPORATED MILK

½ TSP (2 mL) DRIED TARRAGON

MAKE IT!
CREAMY SEAFOOD CHOWDER

Nutrition Facts
Per 1 cup (250 mL)

Amount	% Daily Value
Calories 332	
Fat 8 g	12%
Saturated 2 g + Trans 0 g	9%
Cholesterol 59 mg	20%
Sodium 248 mg	10%
Carbohydrate 34 g	11%
Fibre 3 g	12%
Sugars 13 g	
Protein 27 g	

17%*

* Based on 1,500 mg per day, the amount recommended by Health Canada for those aged 9–50

>soups

A bowl of hot soup soothes the soul. And, needing only a can opener, a microwave and a bowl, it could hardly be easier to prepare. Prepared soups used to be limited to a handful of flavours such as the traditional chicken noodle, tomato and cream of mushroom. Now, prepared soups have gone gourmet with butternut squash, carrot and curry to summer asparagus and sweet basil.

Canned soups are definitely convenient, and often marketed as "healthy," with "health checks" and "increased servings of vegetables." But don't be distracted. Canned soups contain too much salt! Some companies, to their credit, are cutting back on it, but if they cut back even 25 per cent on an amount that was massively too high to begin with, they still have too much salt.

Knorr's Carrot and Coriander Soup may provide 2 servings of vegetables per cup (250 mL), but it also provides a whopping 850 mg of sodium!

That's over half your recommended sodium intake for the entire day! Besides, that one cup (250 mL) of soup is not likely all there will be to your meal; but if you are having a meal only of soup, you'll probably double up on the portion — and double up on the salt!

HOLD IT!
KNORR CARROT & CORIANDER SOUP

Nutrition Facts
Per 1 cup (250 mL)

Amount	% Daily Value
Calories 120	
Fat 6 g	10%
Saturated 3.5 g + Trans 0.1 g	16%
Cholesterol 10 mg	3%
Sodium 850 mg	35%
Carbohydrate 15 g	5%
Fibre 2 g Sugars 6 g	8%
Protein 1 g	

57%*

* Based on 1,500 mg per day, the amount recommended by Health Canada for those aged 9–50

chunky southern soup

MAKES: 6 SERVINGS

TIME: 20 MINUTES TOTAL

This is one of my favourite soups. Believe me, it is bursting with so much flavour that you will not miss the salt. You can use chicken instead of the black beans, or some other legume such as kidney beans or chickpeas. If you do decide to use black beans but can't find them dried, look for canned beans with the lowest sodium content, and be sure to rinse them well before using. Dried chipotle spice can be found at most bulk food stores or in the spice section of some grocery stores, but if you can't track any down, just leave it out. This soup is quite spicy-hot, so if you are sensitive to heat or dislike spicy foods, use only half a pepper and make sure to remove all the seeds.

In a large saucepan over medium-high heat, add oil and sauté garlic, sweet potato and onion for about 5 minutes or until sweet potato begins to soften. Add red or orange pepper, coriander, chili powder, chipotle, lime juice and zest. Continue to sauté for about 3 to 4 minutes. Reduce heat to medium and add broth. Bring to a boil. Reduce heat and add corn, jalapeño and black beans. Add pepper to taste. Simmer for 8 to 10 minutes until sweet potato is tender. Serve topped with 2 slices of avocado per bowl.

1 TSP (5 mL) CANOLA OIL

1 CLOVE GARLIC, MINCED

1 LARGE SWEET POTATO, CHOPPED IN CUBES

1 CUP (250 mL) CHOPPED ONION

1 LARGE RED OR ORANGE PEPPER, SEEDED AND CHOPPED

1 TSP (5 mL) GROUND CORIANDER

½ TBSP (7 mL) CHILI POWDER

1 TSP (5 mL) DRIED CHIPOTLE

JUICE AND ZEST FROM 1 LIME

4 CUPS (1 L) LOW-SODIUM CHICKEN OR VEGETABLE BROTH

1 CUP (250 mL) CORN (FRESH OR FROZEN)

1 JALAPEÑO, SEEDED AND DICED

2 CUPS (500 mL) DRIED BLACK BEANS, PREPARED OR 1 CAN (19 FL OZ/540 G) BLACK BEANS, RINSED

PEPPER TO TASTE

1 AVOCADO, SKIN AND PIT REMOVED

MAKE IT!
CHUNKY SOUTHERN SOUP

Nutrition Facts
Per serving (1/6 of recipe)

Amount	% Daily Value
Calories 227	
Fat 4 g	6%
Saturated 1 g + Trans 0 g	4%
Cholesterol 0 mg	0%
Sodium 85 mg	4%
Carbohydrate 41 g	14%
Fibre 8 g	31%
Sugars 5 g	
Protein 11 g	

6%*

* Based on 1,500 mg per day, the amount recommended by Health Canada for those aged 9–50

apple pumpkin spice soup 🎥

1 TSP (5 ML) CANOLA OIL

2 CLOVES GARLIC, MINCED

1 MEDIUM ONION, DICED

6 CUPS (1.5 L) LOW-SODIUM CHICKEN OR
    VEGETABLE BROTH

3–4 APPLES, PEELED AND DICED

1 CAN (28 FL OZ/796 ML) PURÉED
    PUMPKIN WITHOUT ADDED SPICES

1 1/2 TSP (7 ML) GROUND GINGER

1 TBSP (15 ML) GARAM MASALA

1/2 TSP (2 ML) GROUND CORIANDER

1 1/2 CUPS (375 ML) SKIM MILK

2 TBSP (30 ML) MAPLE SYRUP

PEPPER TO TASTE

6 TBSP (90 ML) LIGHT SOUR CREAM

Garam masala, which means hot spice mixture, is an Indian preparation that may include cumin, peppercorns, cinnamon, nutmeg, cloves and coriander, along with other spices. Its flavour is strong, so a little goes a long way. The apples add a nice fruity flavour and sweetness. You can purée this soup if you prefer a smooth texture. Also, if you prefer a thinner soup, just add more broth or milk to achieve the desired consistency.

In a large saucepan over medium-high heat, add oil and sauté garlic and onion until onion begins to brown. Add broth, apples, pumpkin, ginger, garam masala and coriander. Bring to a boil while stirring constantly. Add milk and maple syrup and return to a boil, then simmer on low heat for 8 to 10 minutes. Add pepper to taste. Serve topped with a tablespoon of sour cream per bowl.

MAKE IT!
APPLE PUMPKIN SPICE SOUP

Nutrition Facts
Per serving (1/6 of recipe)

Amount	% Daily Value
Calories 190	
Fat 4 g	6%
Saturated 2 g + Trans 0 g	8%
Cholesterol 6 mg	2%
Sodium 115 mg	5%
Carbohydrate 33 g	11%
Fibre 5 g	20%
Sugars 20 g	
Protein 9 g	

8%*

* Based on 1,500 mg per day, the amount recommended by Health Canada for those aged 9–50

>couscous salads

Couscous looks like a grain, but it's actually pasta cut into tiny pieces. Now that it's available in whole wheat, I enjoy it even more often; not only for its texture and flavour, but for its convenience. Just pour on boiling water and let it sit for 10 minutes. Though couscous alone is quite bland, unlike rice it readily absorbs added flavours.

Couscous and couscous salad are becoming so popular that you can buy them ready-made or as packaged mixes — commercial products that, unfortunately, are high in salt and fat and made with white couscous rather than whole wheat. And look at that sodium content.

A quarter cup (60 mL) of commercial couscous salad has 450 mg of sodium!

That's 30 per cent of your daily sodium intake. That's far too high for any food, let alone a side dish. In addition, the serving size is unrealistically small.

You can quickly and easily make a delicious couscous salad without the added sodium and fat and load it up with lots of fresh ingredients rather than just boring dry seasonings. Plus, couscous is so versatile. It can be flavoured with vegetables, dried fruits, nuts, seeds, garlic, dill, cayenne, curry . . . the list goes on and on. And this fruit and nut couscous salad has almost no sodium — just 10 mg per 1/2 cup (125 mL). The dill and feta salad has a mere 74 mg. And notice the recipe gives double the serving size of the commercial product.

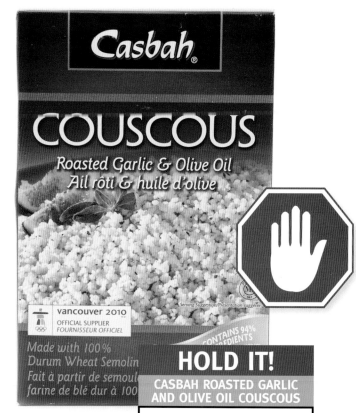

HOLD IT!
CASBAH ROASTED GARLIC
AND OLIVE OIL COUSCOUS

Nutrition Facts	
Per 1/4 cup (60 mL)	
Amount	**% Daily Value**
Calories 160	
Fat 1 g	2%
Saturated 0 g + Trans 0 g	0%
Cholesterol 0 mg	0%
Sodium 450 mg	19%
Carbohydrate 32 g	11%
Fibre 2 g	8%
Sugars 1 g	
Protein 6 g	

30%*

* Based on 1,500 mg per day, the amount recommended by Health Canada for those aged 9–50

dill and feta couscous salad

MAKES: 8 SERVINGS (4 CUPS/1 L)

TIME: 15 MINUTES

This is a great side dish to have with fish, especially salmon or trout, but is also fine with chicken and beef. Feta is quite a salty cheese but here we use just enough to get the flavour without overdoing the sodium. Different versions of feta can contain significantly different levels of sodium, so check those labels and choose the feta that has the least sodium.

Add water to couscous, mix, cover and let stand for 10 minutes. Fluff prepared couscous with a fork then mix in the tomatoes, red pepper and green onions. Add olive oil, dried dill and feta cheese and mix well to combine.

¾ CUP (175 ML) BOILING WATER

1 CUP (250 ML) DRY WHOLE WHEAT COUSCOUS

½ CUP (125 ML) GRAPE TOMATOES, HALVED

1 RED PEPPER, SEEDED AND DICED

2 GREEN ONIONS, CHOPPED

2 TBSP (30 ML) OLIVE OIL

½ TSP (2 ML) DRIED DILL

3 TBSP (45 ML) CRUMBLED FETA CHEESE

MAKE IT!
DILL AND FETA COUSCOUS SALAD

Nutrition Facts
Per 1/2 cup (125 mL)

Amount	% Daily Value
Calories 134	
Fat 5 g	8%
Saturated 1 g + Trans 0 g	7%
Cholesterol 6 mg	2%
Sodium 74 mg	3%
Carbohydrate 18 g	6%
Fibre 2 g	6%
Sugars 1 g	
Protein 4 g	

5%*

* Based on 1,500 mg per day, the amount recommended by Health Canada for those aged 9–50

fruit and nut couscous salad 📹

MAKES: 8 SERVINGS (4 CUPS/1L)

TIME: 15 MINUTES

¾ CUP (175 ML) BOILING WATER

1 CUP (250 ML) DRY WHOLE WHEAT
COUSCOUS

⅓ CUP (75 ML) RED WINE VINEGAR

¼ CUP (60 ML) OLIVE OIL

½ TSP (2 ML) HONEY

½ TSP (2 ML) ORANGE ZEST

JUICE FROM HALF AN ORANGE

A DASH OF CINNAMON

¼ CUP (60 ML) GRAPE TOMATOES,
HALVED

1 CARROT, DICED

¼ CUP (60 ML) DRIED CRANBERRIES

2 TBSP (30 ML) SLIVERED ALMONDS

¼ CUP (60 ML) CHOPPED FRESH
PARSLEY

This is a sweeter couscous, with orange flavours, cranberries and almonds. You might also like to try dried apricots instead of the dried cranberries, and sunflower seeds instead of the almonds. The dash of cinnamon adds a nicely complementary flavour. This is a great salad to enjoy as a side dish or to take to a potluck supper. They'll never guess it's low in sodium!

Add water to couscous, mix, cover and let stand for 10 minutes. Meanwhile, in a small bowl, combine vinegar, oil, honey, orange zest, juice and cinnamon to make a dressing. To finish the salad, fluff the prepared couscous with a fork, mix in the tomatoes, carrot, cranberries, almonds and parsley. Pour on the dressing and stir well to combine.

MAKE IT!
FRUIT AND NUT COUSCOUS SALAD

Nutrition Facts
Per 1/2 cup (125 mL)

Amount	% Daily Value
Calories 153	
Fat 5 g	8%
Saturated 1 g + Trans 0 g	3%
Cholesterol 0 mg	0%
Sodium 10 mg	0%
Carbohydrate 23 g	8%
Fibre 2 g	8%
Sugars 4 g	
Protein 4 g	

0%*

* Based on 1,500 mg per day, the amount recommended by Health Canada for those aged 9–50

>seasoned rice

Packaged seasoned rice makes a quick and tasty side dish that is much more interesting than plain rice. With the range of flavours on the market you can please everyone at the table, and pair the rice up nicely with any main dish. Seasoned rice can even be the basis of a complete meal if you add vegetables and either cut-up chicken or beef, or beans and lentils.

These commercial rice mixes are tasty — but healthy? If you like a little rice with your salt, consider that 1/2 cup (125 mL) of Knorr Vegetable Fried Rice delivers 360 mg of sodium. That's 24 per cent of your recommended sodium for the entire day.

That would be too high for an entire meal, and this is only a side dish! Plus, the serving size is misleadingly small.

There is no need to limit yourself to just plain rice if you're trying to watch your sodium intake, though. The solution is to make your own seasoned rice, from scratch. This will allow you to enjoy seasoned rice that is much tastier than the commercial varieties and has lots of fresh vegetables and herbs.

Once you've eaten such a superior and healthy version, you'll never go back to the packaged product.

HOLD IT!
KNORR VEGETABLE FRIED RICE

Nutrition Facts
Per 1/2 cup (125 mL)

Amount	% Daily Value
Calories 130	
Fat 1 g	2%
Saturated 0.1 g + Trans 0 g	1%
Cholesterol 0 mg	0%
Sodium 360 mg	**15%**
Carbohydrate 26 mg	9%
Fibre 1 g	4%
Sugars 3 g	
Protein 3 g	

24%*

* Based on 1,500 mg per day, the amount recommended by Health Canada for those aged 9–50

vegetable fried rice

MAKES: 5 SERVINGS (5 CUPS/1.3 L)

TIME: 15 MINUTES TOTAL

You can buy the carrot already shredded, if you haven't time to grate your own. Edamame are soy beans with a great buttery flavour, and popular in Japanese cooking. You can buy them frozen, either as pod and beans or as beans only. This recipe uses just the beans. Brown rice takes 30 to 45 minutes to cook so you might decide to use instant brown rice if you're in a hurry. It's not as nutritious as regular brown rice, but it beats white.

In a small bowl, combine oil, vinegar, coriander, ginger, broth, honey, garlic, pepper and the 1/4 cup (60 mL) chopped cilantro. Set aside. In a large non-stick skillet over medium heat, sauté onion and carrot for 4 minutes or until crisp-tender. Add peas, edamame beans and rice and sauté, stirring frequently, until heated through. Pour on the broth mixture and stir to combine. Continue to sauté, turning regularly, for 6 to 8 minutes. Remove from heat and mix in the finely-chopped cilantro. Serve hot or cold.

2 TSP (10 mL) DARK SESAME OIL
2 TBSP (30 mL) RICE VINEGAR
1 TSP (5 mL) GROUND CORIANDER
2 TSP (10 mL) GRATED FRESH GINGER
1/4 CUP (60 mL) LOW-SODIUM CHICKEN BROTH
2 TSP (10 mL) HONEY
2 CLOVES GARLIC, MINCED
1/2 RED CHILI PEPPER, DICED (REMOVE SEEDS IF YOU DISLIKE SPICY FOOD)
1/4 CUP (60 mL) CHOPPED FRESH CILANTRO
6 GREEN ONIONS, CHOPPED
1/2 CUP (125 mL) GRATED CARROT
3/4 CUP (175 mL) FROZEN PEAS, THAWED
3/4 CUP (175 mL) FROZEN EDAMAME BEANS, THAWED
2 1/2 CUPS (625 mL) COOKED BROWN RICE
2 TBSP (30 mL) FINELY CHOPPED CILANTRO

MAKE IT!
VEGETABLE FRIED RICE

Nutrition Facts Per 1 cup (250 mL)	
Amount	**% Daily Value**
Calories 187	
Fat 4 g	6%
Saturated 0 g + Trans 0 g	2%
Cholesterol 0 mg	0%
Sodium 36 mg	2%
Carbohydrate 33 g	11%
Fibre 5 g	18%
Sugars 5 g	
Protein 5 g	

2%*

* Based on 1,500 mg per day, the amount recommended by Health Canada for those aged 9–50

tex-mex rice

MAKES: 4 CUPS (1 L)

TIME: 15 MINUTES

1 ½ CUPS (375 ML) BROWN RICE
(INSTANT BROWN RICE CAN BE USED)*

¾ CUP (175 ML) LOW-SODIUM CHICKEN
BROTH OR WATER

¾ CUP (175 ML) LOW-SODIUM TOMATO
SAUCE

1 TSP (5 ML) VEGETABLE OIL

2 CLOVES GARLIC, MINCED

1 RED PEPPER, SEEDED AND DICED

3 GREEN ONIONS, CHOPPED

1 CAN (12 OZ/341 ML) NO-ADDED-SALT
CORN OR 1 1/2 CUPS (375 ML) FROZEN
CORN, THAWED

1 TOMATO, CHOPPED

½ RED CHILI PEPPER, DICED (REMOVE
SEEDS IF YOU DISLIKE SPICY FOODS)

1 ½ TSP (7 ML) CUMIN

1 ½ TBSP (22 ML) CHILI POWDER

PEPPER TO TASTE

* IF YOU FIND THE RICE IS DRY, ADD
TOMATO SAUCE TO ACHIEVE DESIRED
CONSISTENCY.

Here's an excellent way to add flavour to rice, including some vegetables rich in potassium, the blood-pressure-lowering mineral. The sodium content is only 15 mg per 1/2 cup (125 mL), which is 345 mg less than the packaged product! It's usually a side dish, but you can add chicken or black beans (or both) to make it the centrepiece of a meal.

Prepare the rice as directed on the package, using chicken broth (but only if broth is low-sodium, if it isn't, use water) and tomato sauce. Also, ignore any package instructions to add salt or oil. While rice is cooking, in a large skillet over medium heat add oil and sauté garlic until fragrant, about 30 seconds. Add red pepper and onion and sauté for about 5 minutes. When the rice is cooked, add it to the skillet, along with the corn, tomato, chili pepper, cumin, chili powder and pepper. Mix well and continue to sauté for 10 minutes, stirring frequently.

MAKE IT!
TEX-MEX RICE

Nutrition Facts
Per 1/2 cup (125 mL)

Amount	% Daily Value
Calories 170	
Fat 2 g	3%
Saturated 0 g + Trans 0 g	2%
Cholesterol 0 mg	0%
Sodium 15 mg	<1%
Carbohydrate 35 g	12%
Fibre 2 g	10%
Sugars 2 g	
Protein 4 g	

1%*

* Based on 1,500 mg per day, the amount recommended by Health Canada for those aged 9–50

>french fries

French fries certainly taste good. Not the frozen kind you get from the supermarket or at fast food restaurants, but the ones made from freshly cut potatoes. And sweet potato fries are better still, and equally delicious either baked or deep fried.

Everyone knows that fries are high in fat and salt. I wouldn't say you should never eat fries, but they should certainly be enjoyed in moderation. Just how much sodium is in this tasty treat (not even counting the salt that you sprinkle on, and the ketchup or mayo you might use as a dip)? McCain Superfries Spicy Xtracrispy Straight Cut Fries contain 330 mg of sodium;

! adding the seasoning evidently does come at a price.

Plain French fries are your best choice for commercial fries, at 160 to 260 mg per serving, but they are bland without added salt. Vegetables, naturally low in sodium, should not add salt to your diet.

Now, I will admit that plain baked fries can be quite bland, but all they need to significantly improve the flavour is just a very little salt or perhaps a mixture of spices and herbs. That is exactly what I did to ensure these fries have lots of flavour but remain low in sodium — as potatoes should. Fries no longer have to be enjoyed in moderation. These recipes provide you with a healthy alternative. They do require a little bit more time in the kitchen but they are still quick. Check out the sodium — a mere 44 to 47 mg per serving, and that's with a larger serving size.

HOLD IT!
McCAIN SUPERFRIES XTRACRISPY STRAIGHT CUT FRIES

Nutrition Facts
Per 16 pieces (85 g)

Amount	% Daily Value
Calories 160	
Fat 5 g	8%
Saturated 0.4 g + Trans 0 g	2%
Cholesterol 0 mg	0%
Sodium 330 mg	14% **23%***
Carbohydrate 26 g	9%
Fibre 1 g	4%
Sugars 0 g	
Protein 2 g	

* Based on 1,500 mg per day, the amount recommended by Health Canada for those aged 9–50

spicy fries

MAKES: 6 SERVINGS

TIME: PREPPING 10 MINUTES, COOKING 30 MINUTES

You won't even miss the salt in these fries because the blend of spices provides all the flavour you need. If you like your fries even spicier, add cayenne pepper. The cornmeal delivers the perfect crunch.

Preheat oven to 400°F (200°C). In a large bowl, toss vegetables in olive oil. In a small bowl, combine cornmeal and spices. Pour cornmeal and spice mixture over oiled vegetables and mix to coat. Place on baking sheet and bake for 15 minutes, turn sticks over, and bake for 15 to 20 minutes until slightly browned and tender-crisp.

1 SMALL OR HALF A LARGE TURNIP, PEELED AND CUT INTO MATCHSTICKS ¼ IN (6 MM) THICK

1 MEDIUM SWEET POTATO, CUT INTO STICKS ½ IN (12 MM) THICK

1 MEDIUM POTATO, CUT INTO STICKS ½ IN (12 MM) THICK

2 TSP (10 ML) OLIVE OIL

1 TBSP (15 ML) CORNMEAL

1 TSP (5 ML) ONION POWDER

1 TSP (5 ML) CHILI POWDER

¼ TSP (1 ML) CAYENNE (OPTIONAL)

MAKE IT!
SPICY FRIES

Nutrition Facts
Per serving (105 g)

Amount	% Daily Value
Calories 118	
Fat 3 g	4%
Saturated 0 g + Trans 0 g	2%
Cholesterol 0 mg	0%
Sodium 44 mg	2%
Carbohydrate 23 g	8%
Fibre 3 g	13%
Sugars 3 g	
Protein 3 g	

3%*

* Based on 1,500 mg per day, the amount recommended by Health Canada for those aged 9–50

cinnamon garlic fries ◼◀

MAKES: 4 SERVINGS

TIME: PREPPING 10 MINUTES, COOKING 30 MINUTES

1 MEDIUM TURNIP, PEELED AND CUT
    INTO MATCHSTICKS ¼ IN (3 MM) THICK
1 LARGE SWEET POTATO, CUT INTO
    STICKS ½ IN (12 MM) THICK
2 TSP (10 ML) OLIVE OIL
1 TSP (5 ML) GARLIC POWDER
1 TSP (5 ML) CINNAMON

A hint of cinnamon goes well with both sweet potato and turnip. I will admit, I was a little skeptical when first introduced to turnip fries but after the first bite, I was convinced. Try them! If you're still not a fan just use two sweet potatoes.

Preheat oven to 400°F (200°C). In a large bowl, toss cut-up turnip and sweet potato in olive oil to coat, then toss with garlic and cinnamon. Spread vegetables out on a lightly greased baking sheet or baking stone. Bake for 15 minutes, turn sticks over, and bake for 15 to 20 more minutes until slightly browned and tender-crisp.

MAKE IT!
CINNAMON GARLIC FRIES

Nutrition Facts
Per serving (80 g)

Amount	% Daily Value
Calories 70	
Fat 2 g	4%
Saturated 0 g	2%
+ Trans 0 g	
Cholesterol 0 mg	0%
Sodium 47 mg	2%
Carbohydrate 12 g	4%
Fibre 2 g	8%
Sugars 3 g	
Protein 1 g	

3%*

* Based on 1,500 mg per day, the amount recommended by Health Canada for those aged 9–50

>pasta salads

Pasta is so versatile: it's easy to use in a tasty side salad, and you can prepare pasta salad in a variety of ways by adding different ingredients. You can even add some chicken, seafood or beans, and have a main course.

But pasta salads are usually made with mayonnaise, oil or commercial salad dressing. Unfortunately, these are all high in salt — not to mention fat. It's even a challenge to make a good pasta salad at home without getting too much sodium and fat. Fall for the convenience of picking up a prepared tub of pasta salad in the store or getting macaroni salad as a side at a fast food restaurant, though, and you'll also get a lot of salt. Just how much? Ziggy's Macaroni Salad is a popular brand that comes in a tub at the grocery store.

! A small serving of this salad contains a hefty 450 mg of sodium per 2/3 cup.

This is almost a third of your daily sodium allowance. And keep in mind that it is doubtful whether this salad will make up only a third or a fifth of what you eat during the day, and that you will probably eat more than this modest serving size.

Pasta salad can be a very healthy food when the proper ingredients are used and I assure you there is no comparison in the flavour. The following salads have a larger serving size and still don't contain nearly as much sodium.

HOLD IT!
ZIGGY'S MACARONI SALAD

Nutrition Facts
Per 2/3 cup (150 mL)

Amount	% Daily Value
Calories 190	
Fat 8 g	12%
Saturated 1 g + Trans 0.2 g	6%
Cholesterol 10 mg	3%
Sodium 450 mg	19%
Carbohydrate 26 g	9%
Fibre 2 g	8%
Sugars 4 g	
Protein 3 g	

30%*

* Based on 1,500 mg per day, the amount recommended by Health Canada for those aged 9–50

vegetable, balsamic and goat cheese pasta salad

MAKES: 10 SERVINGS (10 CUPS/2.5 L)

TIME: 15 MINUTES TOTAL

Flavourful balsamic vinegar adds a subtle sweetness to your foods without adding sodium or sugar. Here, it complements the asparagus and goat cheese.

In a large bowl, combine cooked pasta, chopped red pepper, onion and asparagus. In a small bowl, mix goat cheese, vinegar, Dijon and fresh basil. Pour dressing over pasta and mix well until coated.

4 CUPS (1 L) WHOLE WHEAT PASTA, COOKED PER PACKAGE DIRECTIONS, OMITTING ANY OIL OR SALT

2 RED PEPPERS (PREFERABLY ROASTED*), SEEDED AND CHOPPED

½ CUP (125 ML) CHOPPED RED ONION

20 SPEARS ASPARAGUS, STEAMED UNTIL SLIGHTLY TENDER AND CUT INTO 3-IN (7.5-CM) PIECES

½ CUP (125 ML) CRUMBLED GOAT CHEESE

½ CUP (125 ML) BALSAMIC VINEGAR

1 TBSP (15 ML) DIJON MUSTARD

½ CUP (125 ML) COARSELY CHOPPED FRESH BASIL

* FOR DIRECTIONS ON ROASTING PEPPERS, SEE PAGE 40.

MAKE IT!
VEGETABLE, BALSAMIC AND GOAT CHEESE PASTA SALAD

Nutrition Facts
Per 1 cup (250 mL)

Amount	% Daily Value
Calories 188	
Fat 6 g	9%
Saturated 3 g + Trans 0 g	17%
Cholesterol 10 mg	3%
Sodium 112 mg	5%
Carbohydrate 26 g	9%
Fibre 4 g	17%
Sugars 5 g	
Protein 9 g	

7%*

* Based on 1,500 mg per day, the amount recommended by Health Canada for those aged 9–50

maple curry pasta salad

MAKES: 8 SERVINGS (8 CUPS/2 L)

TIME: 16 MINUTES TOTAL

2 ½ CUPS (625 ML) WHOLE WHEAT
   FUSILLI PASTA
2 GREEN PEPPERS, SEEDED AND
   CHOPPED
2 CUPS (500 ML) GRAPE TOMATOES,
   HALVED
½ CUP (125 ML) LOW-FAT PLAIN
   YOGOURT
⅓ CUP (75 ML) LIGHT SOUR CREAM
1 TBSP (15 ML) MAPLE SYRUP
2 TBSP (30 ML) CURRY POWDER
¼ CUP (60 ML) SLIVERED ALMONDS,
   TOASTED*

*TO TOAST YOUR ALMONDS, TOAST IN
   A DRY PAN OVER LOW-MEDIUM HEAT
   UNTIL SLIGHTLY BROWNED.

Sure to be a guest-pleaser, the sweet curry flavour here complements the pasta and almonds. We've cut back the fat by using plain yogourt and light sour cream. Add chicken or shrimp, and you can make it into a meal.

Prepare pasta per package directions but omit any oil and salt. Once pasta is cooked, place in a colander and run under cold water until cooled. In a large bowl, combine cooked pasta, green pepper and tomatoes. In a small bowl, combine yogourt, sour cream, maple syrup and curry powder. Pour dressing over pasta and toss well. Add slivered almonds and combine.

MAKE IT!
MAPLE CURRY PASTA SALAD

Nutrition Facts
Per 1 cup (250 mL)

Amount	% Daily Value
Calories 171	
Fat 4 g	6%
Saturated 1 g + Trans 0 g	6%
Cholesterol 4 mg	1%
Sodium 21 mg	1%
Carbohydrate 30 g	10%
Fibre 4 g	18%
Sugars 5 g	
Protein 7 g	

1%*

* Based on 1,500 mg per day, the amount recommended by Health Canada for those aged 9–50

Condiments,
Dressings,
Sauces and
Seasonings

›condiments

Condiments have become a staple in most kitchens, and there are so many meals people wouldn't consider eating without a splash of ketchup. You wouldn't even think of heading out to the barbecue without the right combination of condiments, right? French fries are the perfect meal for condiment lovers and now come paired with everything from ketchup to gravy to piles of mayo.

! **The unfortunate reality is that these heaped-on condiments also help to pile extra sodium onto your meal.** And often these sauces are paired with foods that are already high in sodium, like burgers and French fries. In just 1 tbsp (15 mL) of Heinz ketchup, for example, you'll consume 140 mg of sodium! That's just too much sodium for a last-minute add-on.

Try these condiment recipes for a healthy way to add extra flavour to your meal. These are easy to make and can be stored in the fridge like the store-bought variety. And best of all, they contain next to no sodium!

HOLD IT!
HEINZ KETCHUP

Nutrition Facts
Per 1 tbsp (15 mL)

Amount	% Daily Value
Calories 20	
Fat 0 g	0%
Saturated 0 g + Trans 0 g	0%
Cholesterol 0 mg	0%
Sodium 140 mg	6%
Carbohydrate 5 g	2%
Fibre 0 g Sugars 5 g	0%
Protein 0.3 g	

9%*

* Based on 1,500 mg per day, the amount recommended by Health Canada for those aged 9–50

ketchup

MAKES: ABOUT 1 1/4 CUPS (310 mL)

TIME: 8 MINUTES

This ketchup may not taste exactly like the bottled variety but it's equally good, tastes great with your French fries and hamburgers, and is healthfully low in sodium. Make sure to check the labels and choose the lowest-sodium tomato paste you can find.

In a small bowl, combine all ingredients. Add more water if a thinner consistency is desired. Store in the refrigerator in an airtight container.

1 CAN (5.5 OZ/165 mL) TOMATO PASTE

1/3 CUP (75 mL) WATER

1/4 CUP (60 mL) VINEGAR

2 TBSP (30 mL) MAPLE SYRUP

1/4 TSP (1 mL) ONION POWDER

1 TSP (5 mL) FRESH OREGANO OR

 1/2 TSP (2 mL) DRIED OREGANO

1 CLOVE GARLIC, MINCED

1/4 TSP (1 mL) MUSTARD POWDER

MAKE IT!

KETCHUP

Nutrition Facts
Per 1 tbsp (15 mL)

Amount	% Daily Value
Calories 13	
Fat 0 g	0%
Saturated 0 g + Trans 0 g	0%
Cholesterol 0 mg	0%
Sodium 9 mg	0%
Carbohydrate 3 g	1%
Fibre 0 g	1%
Sugars 2 g	
Protein 0 g	

0%*

* Based on 1,500 mg per day, the amount recommended by Health Canada for those aged 9-50

bbq sauce

MAKES: 1 CUP (250 mL)

TIME: 8 MINUTES

1 CAN (6 OZ/177 mL) TOMATO PASTE

¼ CUP (60 mL) CIDER VINEGAR

¼ CUP (60 mL) BEER

2 TBSP (30 mL) HONEY OR REDUCED-
SUGAR MOLASSES

2 TBSP (30 mL) BROWN SUGAR

½ TSP (2 mL) MUSTARD POWDER

½ TSP (2 mL) ONION POWDER

1 TBSP (15 mL) CANOLA OIL

This sauce is very easy to prepare and ready in a few minutes. For a smoky flavour add 1/2 tsp (2 mL) of dried chipotle; for spicy add cayenne to taste. This sauce is perfect as is for a marinade but if you are using it as a dip you may want to thin it with water. Adds flavour to meat, poultry, fish or seafood.

In a small bowl, combine all ingredients. Adjust spices and sugar to taste. Store in an airtight container and refrigerate.

MAKE IT!

BBQ SAUCE

Nutrition Facts
Per 1 tbsp (15 mL)

Amount	% Daily Value
Calories 28	
Fat 1 g	1%
Saturated 0 g + Trans 0 g	0%
Cholesterol 0 mg	0%
Sodium 11 mg	<1%
Carbohydrate 5 g	2%
Fibre 0 g	2%
Sugars 4 g	
Protein 0 g	

1%*

* Based on 1,500 mg per day, the amount recommended by Health Canada for those aged 9–50

mint feta spread

MAKES: 1/2 CUP (125 mL)

TIME: 4 MINUTES

½ CUP (125 mL) LOW-FAT PLAIN
 YOGOURT

1 ½ TSP (7 mL) DRIED MINT

¼ TSP (? mL) LEMON ZEST

2 TBSP (30 mL) CRUMBLED FETA

This is similar to the Greek yogourt-based tzatziki sauce but uses lemon and feta cheese to create the refreshing flavour. It's best if you let it rest before serving to allow the tastes to mellow. Spread it on pita bread, or use it as a dip for Greek meatballs (page 114), or for shrimp or chicken skewers.

In a small bowl, combine all ingredients. Store in the refrigerator in an airtight container.

MAKE IT!
MINT FETA SPREAD

Nutrition Facts

Per 2 tbsp (30 mL)

Amount	% Daily Value
Calories 24	
Fat 1 g	1%
Saturated 1 g + Trans 0 g	3%
Cholesterol 4 mg	1%
Sodium 59 mg	2%
Carbohydrate 2 g	1%
Fibre 0 g	0%
Sugars 2 g	
Protein 2 g	

4%*

* Based on 1,500 mg per day, the amount recommended by Health Canada for those aged 9–50

curry mayo

MAKES: 3/4 CUP (75 mL)

TIME: 3 MINUTES

Curry spice adds a lot of flavour without adding salt. This curry mayo is great as a dipping sauce for sweet potato fries or chicken nuggets, or on a burger, or in a sandwich or a wrap, and it is much lower in sodium than either commercial mayonnaise or the commercial curry mayos. If you love spicy foods, you can add heat with some cayenne.

½ CUP (125 mL) LOW-FAT PLAIN YOGOURT
¼ CUP (60 mL) LIGHT SOUR CREAM
½ TSP (2 mL) SUGAR
1 TBSP (15 mL) CURRY POWDER

In a medium bowl, combine all ingredients. Store in the refrigerator in an airtight container.

MAKE IT!
CURRY MAYO

Nutrition Facts
Per 1 tbsp (15 mL)

Amount	% Daily Value
Calories 18	
Fat 1 g	1%
Saturated 1 g + Trans 0 g	3%
Cholesterol 3 mg	1%
Sodium 13 mg	1%
Carbohydrate 2 g	1%
Fibre 0 g	1%
Sugars 1 g	
Protein 1 g	

1%*

* Based on 1,500 mg per day, the amount recommended by Health Canada for those aged 9–50

>pasta sauces

Nothing compares to pasta when you want a hearty, home-cooked meal, and a pasta dish is nothing without a good sauce. Everyone has a favourite — whether tomato, white sauce or rosé, they can all be conveniently purchased in a can or jar. It's all too easy to grab one of the endless variety of ready-made sauces and congratulate yourself for cutting back on a lot of time in the kitchen. Though these store-bought brands sometimes have a reputation for being high in fat, they also contain unnecessary levels of sodium. Classico Alfredo Sauce contains 430 mg sodium per 1/4 cup (60 mL) serving — that's 29 per cent of the recommended daily intake for those aged 9-50. The delicious homemade alfredo sauce presented here contains only about a quarter of the sodium, and this healthy alternative to store-brand sauces doesn't even take much extra time.

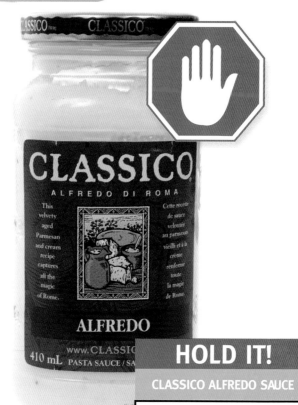

! Those few extra minutes required to prepare a homemade sauce will be worth it for both your heart and your taste buds.

Note that the recipe serving size is more generous, and still proves to be the better option for sodium, calories and fat.

HOLD IT!
CLASSICO ALFREDO SAUCE

Nutrition Facts
Per 1/4 cup (60 mL)

Amount	% Daily Value
Calories 80	
Fat 7 g	11%
Saturated 3.5 g + Trans 0.3 g	20%
Cholesterol 40 mg	13%
Sodium 430 mg	18%
Carbohydrate 3 g	1%
Fibre 0 g	0%
Sugars 2 g	
Protein 1 g	

29%*

* Based on 1,500 mg per day, the amount recommended by Health Canada for those aged 9–50

zesty tomato sauce

MAKES: 6 SERVINGS

TIME: 20 MINUTES

This multipurpose sauce can be used over spaghetti, chicken or seafood. Zest it up by adding your choice of vegetables; sweet peppers, broccoli, cauliflower, spinach and mushrooms all work well. If you love cheese you're in luck because this sauce is so low in sodium that you can top it with a sprinkle of Parmesan or mozzarella cheese and still have a healthy dish.

In a medium saucepan over low-medium heat, add oil and sauté garlic, onion, thyme and chili flakes until fragrant, about 30 seconds. Increase heat to medium, add grape (or cherry) tomatoes, sauté until onion is tender and tomatoes burst. Add wine and broth and bring to a boil. Add tomato sauce and parsley or basil and return to a boil. Simmer over low heat for 8 to 10 minutes, stirring occasionally.

2 TSP (10 ML) OLIVE OIL
2 CLOVES GARLIC, MINCED
1 LARGE ONION, DICED
1/2 TSP (2 ML) THYME
1/4 TO 1/2 TSP (1 TO 2 ML) CHILI FLAKES
1 PINT GRAPE TOMATOES (CAN USE CHERRY INSTEAD)
1/3 CUP (80 ML) WHITE WINE
1/4 CUP (60 ML) LOW-SODIUM CHICKEN BROTH
1 CAN (28 FL OZ/796 ML) NO-ADDED-SALT TOMATO SAUCE
1 TBSP (15 ML) CHOPPED FRESH PARSLEY OR FRESH BASIL

MAKE IT!

ZESTY TOMATO PASTA SAUCE

Nutrition Facts Per 1/2 cup (125 mL)	
Amount	% Daily Value
Calories 68	
Fat 2 g	3%
Saturated 0 g + Trans 0 g	1%
Cholesterol 0 mg	0%
Sodium 13 mg	1%
Carbohydrate 10 g	3%
Fibre 2 g	7%
Sugars 6 g	
Protein 2 g	

1%*

* Based on 1,500 mg per day, the amount recommended by Health Canada for those aged 9–50

vegetable alfredo pasta sauce 📹

MAKES: 4 SERVINGS

TIME: 20 MINUTES TOTAL

Amazingly, there really is a healthy alternative to high-sodium, high-fat alfredo sauce that is still flavourful and has the same creamy-rich consistency. Traditionally, alfredo sauce doesn't include vegetables. Adding them increases the nutrients and adds a nice flavour. If you prefer a plain sauce omit the vegetables. This sauce is great served over your favourite pasta. It's also fabulous with cooked diced chicken or seafood.

In a medium saucepan over low-medium heat, sauté garlic in 1 tsp (5 mL) oil until fragrant, about 30 seconds. Slowly add milk, stirring constantly. Gradually add flour, while constantly whisking to avoid clumping and burning. Cook for about 2 minutes or until thickened. Add Worcestershire sauce, Tabasco, parsley, cream cheese and Parmesan and mix until the cheese is melted and combined. Add pepper to taste. Remove sauce from heat and cover. In a skillet over medium heat, add the remaining 1 tsp (5 mL) oil and sauté red pepper and mushrooms until slightly tender, about 3 minutes. Add spinach and sauté until spinach is wilted. Mix vegetables with the cream sauce and stir in lemon zest and juice and heat to serving temperature.

Serve over spaghettini. If desired, add pepper and garnish with lemon.

---

2 CLOVES ROASTED GARLIC, MINCED OR
  6 CLOVES GARLIC, MINCED
2 TSP (10 mL) CANOLA OIL
1 ½ CUPS (375 mL) SKIM MILK
1 ½ TBSP (22 mL) FLOUR
1 TSP (5 mL) WORCESTERSHIRE SAUCE
1–2 DASHES TABASCO SAUCE
2 TBSP (30 mL) CHOPPED FRESH
  PARSLEY
⅓ CUP (75 mL) LIGHT HERB AND GARLIC
  CREAM CHEESE
3 TBSP (45 mL) GRATED PARMESAN
PEPPER TO TASTE
1 RED PEPPER, SEEDED AND DICED
8 BUTTON MUSHROOMS, SLICED
2 CUPS (500 mL) FRESH, WASHED
  SPINACH
ZEST AND JUICE FROM 1 LEMON

MAKE IT!
ALFREDO PASTA SAUCE

Nutrition Facts
Per 1/2 cup (125 mL)

Amount	% Daily Value
Calories 129	
Fat 6 g	9%
Saturated 3 g + Trans 0 g	13%
Cholesterol 16 mg	5%
Sodium 218 mg	9% 15%*
Carbohydrate 15 g	5%
Fibre 2 g	9%
Sugars 7 g	
Protein 8 g	

* Based on 1,500 mg per day, the amount recommended by Health Canada for those aged 9–50

>salad dressings

There are no limitations to flavour and variety when it comes to salads. The dressing is the last touch that adds the most versatility and flavour. It has the ability to change a salad from Asian flavour to Mediterranean style.

A salad is perceived as a healthy dish but once the dressing is added the nutritional content can take a turn for the worse. There are many options out there and food companies have taken measures to decrease the calories and fat but the sodium content has taken the back burner. The sodium content in most commercial salad dressings is 120 to 200 mg sodium per tbsp. Kraft Balsamic Vinaigrette contains 150 mg sodium per tbsp while the Calorie Wise option contains 190 mg of sodium.

That's 13 per cent of your daily sodium intake if you're aged 9-50. Don't forget this is if you can limit yourself to just a tbsp!

! Considering that dressing is only an unnecessary condiment, the sodium should be much lower.

Omitting dressing from your salad is not the way to go to skip the sodium. The best route: make it from scratch. Homemade dressing is simple to make and you end up with an all-natural product with little to no sodium. The dressings below contain only 1 mg and 31 mg of sodium per tbsp — that's a huge saving! Now you can feel good about choosing a salad!

HOLD IT!
KRAFT CALORIE WISE BALSAMIC VINAIGRETTE

Nutrition Facts
Per 1 tbsp (15 mL)

Amount	% Daily Value
Calories 25	
Fat 2 g	3%
Saturated 0.2 g + Trans 0 g	1%
Cholesterol 0 mg	0%
Sodium 190 mg	8%
Carbohydrate 2 g	1%
Fibre 0 g	0%
Sugars 2 g	
Protein 0.1 g	

13%*

* Based on 1,500 mg per day, the amount recommended by Health Canada for those aged 9–50

buttermilk ranch dressing

MAKES: 3/4 CUP (180 mL)

TIME: 6 MINUTES

This is very like the commercial variety but has much less sodium. You may prefer to thin it out with a bit more water for use on a salad, but I like this consistency for a dip. You can serve it right away, but it will taste better if you let it rest for a few hours in the refrigerator so the flavours can mellow.

In a small bowl, combine all ingredients and mix until well blended. Add water for desired consistency. Refrigerate.

½ CUP (125 mL) BUTTERMILK*

¼ CUP (60 mL) LOW-FAT PLAIN YOGOURT

2 TBSP (30 mL) LIGHT MAYONNAISE

½ TSP (2 mL) LEMON JUICE

¼ TSP (1 mL) MUSTARD POWDER

1 TSP (5 mL) CHOPPED CHIVES

1 TSP (5 mL) DRIED PARSLEY

½ TSP (2 mL) ONION POWDER

½ TSP (2 mL) FRESH DILL

1 TBSP (15 mL) WATER (AS NEEDED)

* TO MAKE BUTTERMILK SUBSTITUTE, COMBINE ½ CUP (125 mL) SKIM MILK WITH ½ TBSP (7 mL) VINEGAR AND LET SIT FOR 5 MINUTES.

MAKE IT!
BUTTERMILK RANCH DRESSING

Nutrition Facts	
Per 1 tbsp (15 mL)	
Amount	**% Daily Value**
Calories 15	
Fat 1 g	1%
Saturated 0 g + Trans 0 g	1%
Cholesterol 2 mg	0%
Sodium 31 mg	1%
Carbohydrate 1 g	0%
Fibre 0 g	0%
Sugars 1 g	
Protein 1 g	

2%*

* Based on 1,500 mg per day, the amount recommended by Health Canada for those aged 9–50

honey mustard dressing

MAKES: 1/2 CUP (125 mL)

TIME: 7 MINUTES

1 CLOVE GARLIC, MINCED

½ TSP (2 mL) MUSTARD POWDER

2 TBSP (30 mL) HONEY

2 TBSP (30 mL) CIDER VINEGAR

1 TBSP (15 mL) WATER

3 TBSP (45 mL) OLIVE OIL

PEPPER TO TASTE

This is my mother's famous salad dressing. It's the perfect dressing for a spinach salad but can also be enjoyed as a sauce for chicken.

In a small bowl, combine all ingredients.

MAKE IT!

HONEY MUSTARD DRESSING

Nutrition Facts	
Per 1 tbsp (15 mL)	
Amount	**% Daily Value**
Calories 62	
Fat 5 g	8%
Saturated 1 g + Trans 0 g	3%
Cholesterol 0 mg	0%
Sodium 1 mg	0%
Carbohydrate 4 g	1%
Fibre 0 g	0%
Sugars 4 g	
Protein 0 g	

0%*

* Based on 1,500 mg per day, the amount recommended by Health Canada for those aged 9–50

balsamic dressing

MAKES: 1/2 CUP (125 mL)

TIME: 7 MINUTES

This balsamic dressing is not only delicious and good for you, but with just a few ingredients required is also very simple to make. This will make a great addition to any salad.

In a small bowl, combine garlic, orange juice, Worcestershire sauce, vinegar, water and brown sugar. Slowly whisk in oil.

1 CLOVE GARLIC, MINCED

JUICE OF 1 ORANGE

1/2 TSP (2 mL) WORCESTERSHIRE SAUCE

3 TBSP (45 mL) BALSAMIC VINEGAR

2 TBSP (30 mL) WATER

1 TBSP (15 mL) BROWN SUGAR

2 TBSP (30 mL) CANOLA OIL

MAKE IT!
BALSAMIC DRESSING

Nutrition Facts	
Per 1 tbsp (15 mL)	
Amount	% Daily Value
Calories 46	
Fat 4 g	5%
Saturated 0 g + Trans 0 g	1%
Cholesterol 0 mg	0%
Sodium 5 mg	0%
Carbohydrate 3 g	1%
Fibre 0 g	0%
Sugars 3 g	
Protein 0 g	

0%*

* Based on 1,500 mg per day, the amount recommended by Health Canada for those aged 9–50

›seasoning mixes

A good seasoning mix adds that little something extra to any dish or snack, and can completely change the flavour of meat. It is easy to buy these mixes ready-made at any grocery store and transform a simple dish into restaurant-quality fare.

A quick glance at the nutritional labels of these store-brand seasoning mixes, though, will convince you that they come packed with as much sodium as they do flavour.

Take Club House's brand of Montreal Steak Spice, for example. In just a 1/2-tsp (1-mL) serving you'll have consumed 13 per cent of your recommended daily intake. That may not seem like much, but it's a lot for a little bit of seasoning!

Fortunately, it only takes a few minutes in the kitchen to create your own tasty seasoning mixes for a variety of purposes. These homemade meal add-ons will keep you from adding on extra sodium too, even with a serving size twice as large as the store-bought spice.

HOLD IT!
CLUB HOUSE MONTREAL STEAK SPICE

Nutrition Facts
Per 1/2 tsp (1 g)

Amount	% Daily Value
Calories 0	
Fat 0 g	0%
Saturated 0 g + Trans 0 g	0%
Cholesterol 0 mg	0%
Sodium 200 mg	9%
Carbohydrate 0 mg	0%
Fibre 0 g Sugars	0%
Protein 0.1 g	

13%*

* Based on 1,500 mg per day, the amount recommended by Health Canada for those aged 9–50

bbq spice mix

MAKES: 1/2 CUP (125 mL)

TIME: 3 MINUTES

Low-sodium herb and spice mixes are an easy way to add flavour to that bland chicken breast or make a great replacement for the saltshaker at the table. The BBQ spice mix is a great replacement for steak spice or a Cajun mix. It adds a little heat to your food but you can cut back or omit the cayenne. Both herb and spice mixes taste great on chicken, pork, steak or shrimp. You can also use it as rub and allow it to marinate for a few hours or overnight.

Combine all ingredients. Store in an airtight container.

3 TBSP (45 mL) BROWN SUGAR
1 ½ TBSP (22 mL) CHILI POWDER
1 ½ TBSP (22 mL) PAPRIKA
1 TBSP (15 mL) CUMIN
½ TSP (2 mL) CAYENNE
1 TBSP (15 mL) GARLIC POWDER
1 TBSP (15 mL) MUSTARD POWDER
FRESH GROUND PEPPER

MAKE IT!
BBQ SPICE MIX

Nutrition Facts
Per 1 tsp (5 mL)

Amount	% Daily Value
Calories 13	
Fat 0 g	0%
Saturated 0 g + Trans 0 g	0%
Cholesterol 0 mg	0%
Sodium 6 mg	0%
Carbohydrate 3 g	1%
Fibre 0 g	2%
Sugars 2 g	
Protein 0 g	

0%*

* Based on 1,500 mg per day, the amount recommended by Health Canada for those aged 9–50

herb and spice mix

MAKES: 1/4 CUP (60 ML)

TIME: 3 MINUTES

1 ½ TBSP (22 ML) ONION POWDER

2 TSP (10 ML) GARLIC POWDER

2 TSP (10 ML) PAPRIKA

2 TSP (10 ML) MUSTARD POWDER

1 TSP (5 ML) DRIED THYME

1 TSP (5 ML) DRIED BASIL

½ TSP (2 ML) DRIED ROSEMARY

½ TSP (2 ML) CRACKED BLACK PEPPER

This herb and spice mix is a perfect complement to most foods, including vegetables, pork, beef or chicken. Add it prior to, during or after you cook your protein of choice. It's added flavour made simple!

Combine all ingredients. Store in an airtight container.

MAKE IT!

HERB AND SPICE MIX

Nutrition Facts

Per 1 tsp (5 mL)

Amount	% Daily Value
Calories 8	
Fat 0 g	0%
Saturated 0 g	0%
+ Trans 0 g	
Cholesterol 0 mg	0%
Sodium 1 mg	0%
Carbohydrate 1 g	0%
Fibre 0 g	1%
Sugars 0 g	
Protein 0 g	

0%*

* Based on 1,500 mg per day, the amount recommended by Health Canada for those aged 9–50

Main Dishes

›fajitas

I'm a big fan of spicy foods and I love Mexican. You can adjust the spiciness to your liking and it still has lots of flavour. Take fajitas and burritos, for example: hot vegetables, meat and seasonings, wrapped in a tortilla, topped with salsa and sour cream — delicious!

Even if you buy the elements separately and make your own,

! one large chicken fajita with seasoning mix, salsa and sour cream has about 1,350 mg of sodium.

That's 90 per cent of your recommended amount for the entire day. The right combination of vegetables, meat and seasonings provides all the flavour you need. Chicken fajitas made from the recipe that follows are a great source of potassium, a good source of fibre, lower in fat than the commercial versions and, amazingly, contain only 62 mg of sodium per 2 fajitas! By making these you can avoid 1,285 mg of sodium, effortlessly. You'd be wise to do without a sour cream topping but salsa is a must, and I would suggest making your own (see recipe on page 51). In a pinch, though, if you buy bottled salsa, compare the labels, pick the one with the least sodium and limit your serving size. To avoid the high sodium in commercial flour tortillas, I'd recommend making your own or using corn tortillas. There's a recipe on page 34.

OLD EL PASO Fajita Kit

20

Just Add:
1 lb (500 g) Boneless Chicken or Beef
1 Green or Red Pepper
1 Onion
Toppings

Kit Includes:
12 Soft Tortillas

470 g SERVING SUGGESTION

HOLD IT!

OLD EL PASO FAJITA KIT

Nutrition Facts	
Per 2 tortillas, mix & sauce	
Amount	**% Daily Value**
Calories 190	
Fat 5 g	7%
Saturated 1 g + Trans 1.5 g	5%
Cholesterol 0 mg	0%
Sodium 950 mg	48%
Carbohydrate 32 g	11%
Fibre 1 g	4%
Sugars 2 g	
Protein 4 g	

63%*

* Based on 1,500 mg per day, the amount recommended by Health Canada for those aged 9–50

chicken fajitas 🎥

MAKES: 6 SERVINGS

TIME: PREPPING 15 MINUTES, COOKING 10 MINUTES

This is a Mexican-inspired recipe from my friend Heather, who lived in that country for several years. These fajitas are quick to prepare, are delicious and have delightfully different sweet maple and oregano flavour overtones.

In a medium bowl, combine oil, maple syrup, vinegar, garlic, oregano and cayenne. Add sliced chicken and mix to coat. Set aside to marinate while you prepare the vegetables. In a large skillet over medium-high heat, cook chicken and marinade until chicken is white on all sides but not cooked through. Add peppers, tomatoes and onion and continue to sauté until chicken is cooked and vegetables are slightly tender. Warm corn/flour tortillas in the microwave for a few seconds to soften. Divide filling mixture into portions and wrap in tortillas, topped with salsa. If using flour tortillas, cut each in half.

2 TBSP (30 mL) VEGETABLE OIL
2 TBSP (30 mL) MAPLE SYRUP
1 TBSP (15 mL) RED WINE VINEGAR
2 CLOVES GARLIC, MINCED
2 TSP (10 mL) DRIED OREGANO
½ TSP (2 mL) CAYENNE
3 SMALL CHICKEN BREASTS OR 3 CHICKEN BREAST HALVES, SLICED
1 RED PEPPER, SEEDED AND THINLY SLICED
1 GREEN PEPPER, SEEDED AND THINLY SLICED
2 PLUM TOMATOES, CHOPPED
1 ONION, THINLY SLICED
12 CORN TORTILLAS OR 6 FLOUR TORTILLAS (PAGE 34)
SALSA (PAGE 51)

MAKE IT!
CHICKEN FAJITAS

Nutrition Facts
Per 2 fajitas

Amount	% Daily Value
Calories 245	
Fat 7 g	10%
Saturated 1 g + Trans 0 g	4%
Cholesterol 32 mg	11%
Sodium 62 mg	3%
Carbohydrate 31 g	10%
Fibre 4 g	17%
Sugars 7 g	
Protein 16 g	

4%*

* Based on 1,500 mg per day, the amount recommended by Health Canada for those aged 9–50

>stir-fry

Stir-fry is such a popular dish because it's so easy to adjust the ingredients to suit anyone's taste. It's a delicious way to prepare vegetables and meat together with your favourite sauces (without a lot of mess) for a healthy and satisfying meal.

Be careful if you use a store-bought sauce to make that stir-fry, though. VH Orange Ginger Stir-Fry Sauce, for example has

! 790 mg of sodium in just 100 mL!

Some vegetables with your salt? Not to mention 9 tsp (45 mL) of sugar!

This is over half your recommended daily sodium intake if you're between 9-50. Remember, this is just for the sauce alone!

You can keep this dish healthy by taking a few extra minutes to prepare your own stir-fry. This delicious recipe is both easy to make and low in sodium.

HOLD IT!
VH ORANGE GINGER STIR FRY SAUCE

Nutrition Facts
Per 2/5 cup (100 mL)

Amount	% Daily Value
Calories 180	
Fat 0 g	0%
Saturated 0 g + Trans 0 g	0%
Cholesterol 0 mg	0%
Sodium 790 mg	33% **53%***
Carbohydrate 44 g	15%
Fibre 1 g Sugars 35 g	4%
Protein 0.4 g	

* Based on 1,500 mg per day, the amount recommended by Health Canada for those aged 9–50

cashew mango chicken stir-fry

MAKES: 6 SERVINGS

TIME: PREPPING 10 MINUTES, COOKING 15 MINUTES

Mango and coconut milk, not the customary sodium-laced soy sauce, provide the flavour punch in this delicious stir-fry. You can certainly use fresh vegetables rather than frozen, but they will take a bit longer to prepare and to cook. Serve this stir-fry over rice, whole wheat noodles or couscous.

In a bowl, combine coconut milk, pineapple juice, ginger and soy sauce and add flour, whisking well so flour doesn't clump. In a large non-stick skillet, heat 1 tsp (5 mL) of the oil over medium heat. Add chicken breast slices and sauté until just cooked and no longer pink. Remove from pan and set aside. In the same skillet, heat the other 1 tsp (5 mL) oil over medium heat. Add garlic and sauté until fragrant, about 30 seconds. Add onion and green pepper and sauté for 2 to 3 minutes. Add frozen vegetables and sauté until heated through. Add sauce, chicken and cashews to skillet and sauté for several minutes until sauce has thickened. Add mango and cook for 2 minutes. Add pepper to taste. Serve over cooked rice.

½ CUP (125 ML) LIGHT COCONUT MILK
¾ CUP (175 ML) PINEAPPLE JUICE
½ TBSP (7 ML) MINCED FRESH GINGER
½ TBSP (7 ML) SOY SAUCE
1 TBSP (15 ML) FLOUR
2 TSP (10 ML) CANOLA OIL
2 SKINLESS, BONELESS CHICKEN BREASTS, FAT REMOVED, SLICED
2 CLOVES GARLIC, MINCED
1 ONION, THINLY SLICED
1 GREEN PEPPER, SLICED
6 CUPS (1.5 L) FRESH OR FROZEN STIR-FRY VEGETABLES
3 TBSP CASHEWS
1 RIPE MANGO, PEELED, PITTED AND CHOPPED
PEPPER TO TASTE

MAKE IT!
CASHEW MANGO CHICKEN STIR FRY

Nutrition Facts
Per serving (1/6 of recipe)

Amount	% Daily Value
Calories 357	
Fat 4 g	7%
Saturated 1 g + Trans 0 g	5%
Cholesterol 23 mg	8%
Sodium 142 mg	6%
Carbohydrate 64 g	21%
Fibre 10 g	38%
Sugars 10 g	
Protein 18 g	

9%*

* Based on 1,500 mg per day, the amount recommended by Health Canada for those aged 9–50

›chicken nuggets

McDonald's does have the best chicken nuggets but, to be honest, I'd also settle for the frozen type. Now you can even get lower-fat varieties. Unless you make your own, though, chicken in this form should be only an occasional treat, because all "convenience" nuggets are high in sodium. McDonald's box of 6 nuggets, for example, contains 670 mg of sodium, which makes up 45 per cent of the recommended daily amount of sodium.

! A smaller serving of 4 President's Choice Blue Menu nuggets still contains 460 mg of sodium,

which is 31 per cent of the recommended daily amount. Why consume all that sodium when you can follow these recipes for a healthier meal?

The homemade version is delicious and allows you to add tasty variations such as spices and herbs to your recipe. One of the recipes contains only 92 to 120 mg of sodium.

35% LESS FAT THAN PC® CHICKEN NUGGETS
35 % MOINS DE GRAS QUE LES PÉPITES DE POULET PC®

BLUE MENU BLEU

New! Nouveau!

breaded cutlettes · uncooked
Chicken Nuggets
Pépites de poulet
escalopettes panées · non cuites

1 kg   38 PIECES MORCEAUX   MADE WITH WHITE BREAST MEAT FAITES DE LA VIANDE BLANCHE DE POITRINE

HOLD IT!
PC BLUE MENU CHICKEN NUGGETS

Nutrition Facts
Per 4 nuggets (100 g)

Amount	% Daily Value
Calories 190	
Fat 8 g	12%
Saturated 1 g + Trans 0 g	5%
Cholesterol 15 mg	5%
Sodium 460 mg	19%
Carbohydrate 18 g	6%
Fibre 1 g	4%
Sugars 5 g	
Protein 12 g	

31%*

* Based on 1,500 mg per day, the amount recommended by Health Canada for those aged 9–50

rosemary and parmesan tenders

MAKES: 4 SERVINGS (5 TENDERS EACH)

TIME: PREPPING 10 MINUTES, COOKING 10 TO 12 MINUTES

These are great to eat plain, dipped in a sauce, as part of a salad or inside a wrap. There are several varieties of low-sodium, low-fat crackers you can choose from. I use Breton brand, but you might prefer one of the others. Pick your own favourite dipping sauce but if it's a commercial brand, just be careful about the sodium content.

Preheat oven to 400°F (200°C). In a medium bowl, immerse chicken pieces in buttermilk or orange juice. Make sure chicken is covered. Set aside to marinate until other prep is complete. In a freezer bag, combine crushed crackers, rosemary, onion powder, garlic powder, paprika, cheese and pepper. Remove chicken from buttermilk/orange juice and shake off any excess liquid. Place all chicken pieces in bag with cracker mixture and shake until chicken is coated. Remove chicken pieces and place on a baking sheet. Bake for 10 to 12 minutes, until juices are clear when you cut into the centre of a piece. Serve with sweet and sour sauce, honey, ketchup (page 81) or BBQ sauce (page 82).

2 BONELESS CHICKEN BREASTS, EACH BREAST CHOPPED INTO 10 PIECES

½ CUP (125 ML) BUTTERMILK* OR ORANGE JUICE

6 TBSP (90 ML) CRUSHED REDUCED-SODIUM CRACKERS (I USE BRETON REDUCED-FAT AND REDUCED-SODIUM CRACKERS)

1 TSP (5 ML) DRIED ROSEMARY

½ TSP (2 ML) ONION POWDER

1 TSP (5 ML) GARLIC POWDER

1 TSP (5 ML) PAPRIKA

1 TBSP (15 ML) GRATED PARMESAN

½ TSP PEPPER

* TO MAKE BUTTERMILK SUBSTITUTE, COMBINE 1 CUP (250 ML) SKIM MILK WITH 1 TBSP (15 ML) VINEGAR AND LET SIT FOR 5 MINUTES.

MAKE IT!
ROSEMARY AND
PARMESAN TENDERS

Nutrition Facts
Per 5 tenders

Amount	% Daily Value
Calories 125	
Fat 3 g	5%
Saturated 0 g + Trans 0 g	0%
Cholesterol 35 mg	12%
Sodium 120 mg	5%
Carbohydrate 7 g	2%
Fibre 0 g	0%
Sugars 1 g	
Protein 17 g	

8%*

* Based on 1,500 mg per day, the amount recommended by Health Canada for those aged 9–50

asian sesame chicken nuggets

MAKES: 4 SERVINGS (5 NUGGETS EACH)

TIME: PREPPING 10 MINUTES, COOKING 10 TO 12 MINUTES

Try these, for a change. Ginger and sesame seeds provide an interesting Asian flavour. Use cracker crumbs or panko for that crisp coating. To add some colour to these nuggets, use black sesame seeds instead. For a dipping sauce, use commercial plum sauce or, better yet, our curry mayo (page 85) or ketchup (page 81).

½ CUP (125 ML) BUTTERMILK* OR ORANGE JUICE

2 TSP (10 ML) MINCED FRESH GINGER

2 BONELESS CHICKEN BREASTS, EACH BREAST CHOPPED INTO 10 PIECES

6 TBSP (90 ML) CRUSHED REDUCED-SODIUM CRACKERS (I USE BRETON REDUCED-FAT AND REDUCED-SODIUM CRACKERS)

1 TBSP (15 ML) TOASTED SESAME SEEDS**

½ TSP (2 ML) CHILI PEPPER FLAKES (IF YOU LIKE SPICY FOODS, DOUBLE THIS QUANTITY)

1 TSP (5 ML) GARLIC POWDER

1 TSP (5 ML) CUMIN

½ TSP (2 ML) GROUND CORIANDER

PEPPER TO TASTE

Place baking sheet in oven and preheat oven to 400°F (200°C). In a medium bowl, combine buttermilk/orange juice and ginger. Immerse chicken pieces in buttermilk or orange juice. Make sure chicken is covered. Set aside to marinate until other prep is complete. In a freezer bag, combine crushed crackers, sesame seeds, chili flakes, garlic, cumin, coriander and pepper. Remove chicken from buttermilk/orange juice and shake off any excess liquid. Place all chicken pieces in bag with cracker mixture and shake until chicken is coated. Remove chicken pieces and place on the hot baking sheet once removed from oven. Bake for 10 to 12 minutes, until juices are clear when you cut into the centre of a piece. Serve with sauce of your choice, such as sweet and sour, curry or honey.

* TO MAKE BUTTERMILK SUBSTITUTE, COMBINE ½ CUP (125 ML) SKIM OR MILK WITH 1/2 TBSP (7 ML) VINEGAR AND LET SIT FOR 5 MINUTES.

** TO QUICKLY TOAST SESAME SEEDS, SAUTÉ IN A DRY SKILLET OVER MEDIUM HEAT FOR 5 MINUTES OR UNTIL SLIGHTLY BROWNED.

MAKE IT!
ASIAN SESAME CHICKEN NUGGETS

Nutrition Facts
Per 5 nuggets

Amount	% Daily Value
Calories 166	
Fat 4 g	6%
Saturated 0 g + Trans 0 g	0%
Cholesterol 35 mg	12%
Sodium 92 mg	4% 6%*
Carbohydrate 10 g	3%
Fibre 1 g	4%
Sugars 2 g	
Protein 16 g	

* Based on 1,500 mg per day, the amount recommended by Health Canada for those aged 9–50

>chili

Chili, that beloved mixture of beans, meat and tomatoes, can be paired with rice or a slice of bread to provide something from every food group. That's a complete meal! But canned chili or chili from a fast food restaurant may also be loaded with sodium (and fat, including saturated fat) along with its nutrients. One cup (250 mL) of Stagg Chili (a little over half a can) contains 810 mg of sodium! If you usually eat all the chili in a can (about 1 3/4 cups/425 mL), you're eating 1,393 mg of sodium. That's 93 per cent of the allowance for the whole day. (And a cup of Stagg Chili also gives you 320 calories, 16 g of fat and 7 g of saturated fat. The other brands are similar.) Tim Horton's chili has 1,320 mg of sodium, Wendy's large size has 1,310 mg.

You can make a fine chili that tastes just as good as that salty competition, and it's easy to prepare. It also freezes well. And the sodium?

! To get as much sodium as you'd get from just one can of Stagg, you'd have to eat nearly 10 lbs (4.4 kg, to be exact) of this bean and turkey chili!

HOLD IT!
STAGG CLASSIC CHILI

Nutrition Facts
Per 1 cup (247 g)

Amount	% Daily Value
Calories 320	
Fat 16 g	25%
Saturated 7 g + Trans 1 g	35%
Cholesterol 40 mg	13%
Sodium 810 mg	34%
Carbohydrate 28 g	9%
Fibre 7 g	28%
Sugars 6 g	
Protein 16 g	

54%*

* Based on 1,500 mg per day, the amount recommended by Health Canada for those aged 9–50

bean and turkey chili 🎥

MAKES: 4 TO 6 SERVINGS

TIME: PREPPING 15 MINUTES, COOKING 30 MINUTES

You can easily make this vegetarian by omitting the turkey and increasing the beans to 3 cups (750 mL). If you prefer a spicier version, just add a dash of cayenne. This chili is great served over brown rice or with pita chips (pages 43 and 44).

In a non-stick skillet over medium heat, sauté turkey until cooked and no longer pink. Remove from skillet and place in a strainer. Rinse under warm water to remove excess fat. In a saucepan, heat oil over medium-high heat and sauté garlic until fragrant, about 30 seconds. Add green pepper, onion and jalapeño and sauté until slightly tender, about 2 minutes. Add chili powder, cumin and oregano and sauté for about 30 seconds. Add tomatoes and beans, mix, bring to a boil and cook for 2 minutes. Mix in molasses. Reduce heat to low and simmer uncovered for about 30 minutes or until preferred consistency is reached (chili will thicken as it cooks). If desired, top with light sour cream and chopped green onion.

8 OZ (230 G) EXTRA-LEAN GROUND TURKEY

1 TSP (5 ML) VEGETABLE OIL

3 CLOVES GARLIC, MINCED

1 LARGE GREEN PEPPER, SEEDED AND CHOPPED

1 MEDIUM ONION, DICED

1 JALAPEÑO, SEEDED AND DICED

2 TBSP (30 ML) CHILI POWDER

1 ½ TSP (7 ML) CUMIN

1 TSP (5 ML) DRIED OREGANO

1 CAN (28 FL OZ/796 ML) NO-ADDED-SALT DICED TOMATOES WITH JUICE

2 CUPS (500 ML) KIDNEY BEANS, COOKED OR CANNED

1 TBSP (15 ML) REDUCED-SUGAR MOLASSES (OPTIONAL)

SOUR CREAM (OPTIONAL)

GREEN ONION, CHOPPED (OPTIONAL)

MAKE IT!
BEAN AND TURKEY CHILI

Nutrition Facts
Per serving (1 cup)

Amount	% Daily Value
Calories 167	
Fat 4 g	6%
Saturated 1 g + Trans 0 g	5%
Cholesterol 30 mg	10%
Sodium 51 mg	2%
Carbohydrate 22 g	7%
Fibre 6 g	24%
Sugars 5 g	
Protein 13 g	

3%*

* Based on 1,500 mg per day, the amount recommended by Health Canada for those aged 9–50

›shake 'n bake chicken

There is a reason that Shake 'n Bake has been around for so long: why bother with plain, boring chicken when you can quickly add a tasty premade seasoning mix coating? It's simply a classic and enjoyable way to add a lot of flavour to your chicken.

Shake 'n Bake tastes fine, certainly, but is it the healthiest choice? Unfortunately, as with most convenience foods, much of the flavour in this seasoning mix comes from added sodium.

! With sodium being in the top 5 ingredients, it's no wonder this seasoning is so tasty.

The nutritional facts tell it all: a serving of 1/6 of the seasoning mix package contains 320 mg of sodium! This is 21 per cent of your sodium intake for the day, just from the seasoning alone.

If you had a good recipe that required only a few additional minutes to prepare and you could save on the sodium, would you throw Shake 'n Bake to the curb? "Flavourful" and "convenient" do not have to mean "unhealthy." Herbs and spices provide all the flavour you need and, yes, without the salt. At only 188 mg of sodium, this recipe contains almost half the sodium than the commercial type — and that includes the chicken!

HOLD IT!

SHAKE 'N BAKE ORIGINAL

Nutrition Facts
Per 1/6 pouch (12 g)

Amount	% Daily Value
Calories 45	
Fat 1 g	2%
Saturated 0.4 g + Trans 0 g	2%
Cholesterol 0 mg	0%
Sodium 320 mg	13%
Carbohydrate 8 g	3%
Fibre 0 g	0%
Sugars 0 g	
Protein 1 g	

21%*

* Based on 1,500 mg per day, the amount recommended by Health Canada for those aged 9–50

zippy 'n zesty chicken thighs

MAKES: 6 SERVINGS

TIME: PREPPING 12 MINUTES, COOKING 25 MINUTES

I'd be lying if I said that coming up with a low-sodium herb and spice mixture comparable to Shake 'n Bake was easy. But, after a fair amount of experimenting and testing, this recipe seems just about right. It has a lot of flavour and the same crispy texture. If you are like me and have a need for spice, include the cayenne. If not, the other herbs and spices still provide lots of flavour. You can use this mixture to coat drumsticks, chicken breasts or pork loins. These are great served with homemade spicy fries (page 73).

1/2 CUP (125 ML) BUTTERMILK* OR ORANGE JUICE
2 CLOVES GARLIC, MINCED
12 CHICKEN THIGHS, SKIN REMOVED
1/2 CUP (125 ML) PANKO OR CRUSHED LOW-SODIUM CRACKERS
2 TBSP (30 ML) CHILI POWDER
1 TSP (5 ML) ONION POWDER
1 TSP (5 ML) CUMIN
1 1/2 TSP (7 ML) SUGAR
1/2 TO 1 TSP (2 TO 5 ML) CAYENNE (OPTIONAL)

* TO MAKE BUTTERMILK SUBSTITUTE, COMBINE 1/2 CUP (125 ML) SKIM MILK WITH 1/2 TBSP (7 ML) VINEGAR AND LET SIT FOR 5 MINUTES.

Preheat oven to 375°F (190°C). In a shallow dish, mix together buttermilk or orange juice and garlic. Lay chicken in and turn to coat. Place in refrigerator until other prep is completed. In a large bag, combine panko, chili powder, onion powder, cumin, sugar and cayenne (optional). Remove chicken from buttermilk/ orange juice, place 4 thighs in the bag at a time, and shake to coat. Continue until all chicken is coated. Place coated chicken on a baking sheet. Bake for 25 minutes or until juices are clear when you cut into the centre of the piece.

MAKE IT!
ZIPPY 'N ZESTY CHICKEN THIGHS

Nutrition Facts
Per 2 thighs

Amount	% Daily Value
Calories 178	
Fat 8 g	13%
Saturated 2 g + Trans 0 g	11%
Cholesterol 60 mg	20%
Sodium 96 mg	4% 6%*
Carbohydrate 8 g	3%
Fibre 1 g	4%
Sugars 2 g	
Protein 18 g	

* Based on 1,500 mg per day, the amount recommended by Health Canada for those aged 9–50

›curry

Ethnic foods are becoming more and more popular and curries are certainly one of the favourites.

Curry is a great way to add a lot of flavour and a little spice to a meal without adding a lot of unwanted sodium.

Check out the label of store-bought curry sauce, however, and you'll be in for a surprise.

! **In just one serving of Lee Kum Kee curry sauce you'll consume 1,220 mg of sodium — almost the total recommended daily amount for people between the ages of 9 and 50.**

Why consume this much sodium in a store-bought sauce when you can make your own tasty sauce that's healthy too? The curry sauce in this recipe provides all the flavour you look for without overloading on sodium. It contains only 143 mg of sodium for the sauce plus the chicken, only 9 per cent of your recommended sodium intake. That's 143 mg compared to 1,220 mg of sodium — need I say more?

HOLD IT!

LEE KUM KEE CURRY SAUCE

Nutrition Facts
Per 1 1/2 tbsp (23 mL)

Amount	% Daily Value
Calories 70	
Fat 4.5 g	7%
Saturated 1.5 g + Trans 0.2 g	9%
Cholesterol 0 mg	0%
Sodium 1220 mg	51%
Carbohydrate 7 g	2%
Fibre 1 g	4%
Sugars 5 g	
Protein 1 g	

81%*

* Based on 1,500 mg per day, the amount recommended by Health Canada for those aged 9–50

curry peanut chicken

MAKES: 6 SERVINGS

TIME: 25 MINUTES TOTAL

This recipe proves that you don't need those bottled curry sauces to make a tasty meal. This chicken is great over brown rice or whole wheat couscous. Instead of drumsticks you could use chicken breast, or you could make it vegetarian by using tofu or prepared chickpeas and low-sodium vegetable broth. If you choose to use canned chickpeas, they are going to be higher in sodium. Just make sure to rinse and drain them well.

In a skillet, heat oil. Add onion and garlic and cook for several minutes until onion is tender. Stir in curry powder, cinnamon and peanut butter. Cook until fragrant and peanut butter is melted. Add chicken to skillet and cook for several minutes until no longer pink. Add broth and reduce heat to low. Allow to cook for about 10 minutes until chicken is cooked through and juices are clear. Remove from heat and mix in yogourt. Top each serving with parsley.

1 TSP (5 mL) OLIVE OIL

1 LARGE ONION, SLICED

2 CLOVES GARLIC, MINCED

2 TBSP (30 mL) CURRY POWDER

½ TSP (2 mL) CINNAMON

2 TBSP (30 mL) PEANUT BUTTER

12 CHICKEN DRUMSTICKS, SKIN REMOVED

¼ CUP (175 mL) LOW-SODIUM CHICKEN BROTH

½ CUP (125 mL) LOW-FAT PLAIN YOGOURT

3 TBSP (45 mL) CHOPPED FRESH PARSLEY

MAKE IT!
CURRY PEANUT CHICKEN

Nutrition Facts
Per 2 drumsticks

Amount	% Daily Value
Calories 214	
Fat 8 g	12%
Saturated 2 g + Trans 0 g	10%
Cholesterol 60 mg	20%
Sodium 143 mg	6%
Carbohydrate 15 g	5%
Fibre 2 g	8%
Sugars 5 g	
Protein 21 g	

9%*

* Based on 1,500 mg per day, the amount recommended by Health Canada for those aged 9–50

>meatballs

Meatballs change character dramatically depending on the sauce you put on them. Teriyaki, sweet and sour and BBQ are only some of the possibilities. Buy frozen meatballs with sauce, and all you have to do is put them in the oven and bake.

Commercial meatballs are convenient, but are usually rubbery from the fillers they contain.

And 6 of those small meatballs deliver as much as 310 mg of sodium

— that's 21 per cent of the recommended daily amount for people aged 9-50. That sodium had to be virtually all added in processing, because ground meat is not naturally high in sodium.

Meatballs do take a little bit of time to prepare at home, but yours will have both less sodium and a more pleasing texture than the commercial varieties. And you control what meat goes into them.

HOLD IT!
PRESIDENT'S CHOICE BLUE MENU LEAN ITALIAN BEEF MEATBALLS

Nutrition Facts
Per 6 meatballs (85 g)

Amount	% Daily Value
Calories 160	
Fat 8 g	12%
Saturated 4.5 g + Trans 0.3 g	24%
Cholesterol 55 mg	18%
Sodium 310 mg	13%
Carbohydrate 7 g	2%
Fibre 1 g	4%
Sugars 0 g	
Protein 15 g	

21%*

* Based on 1,500 mg per day, the amount recommended by Health Canada for those aged 9–50

BLUE MENU BLEU

50% LESS FAT THAN PC® ITALIAN BEEF MEATBALLS   50 % MOINS DE GRAS QUE LES BOULETTES DE BŒUF ITALIENNES PC®

READY IN 1½ MIN. ET C'EST PRÊT

Lean Italian
beef meatballs · fully cooked · product of U.S.A.
boulettes de bœuf · cuites à fond · produit des É.-U.A.
Italiennes · Maigres

Improved! Amélioré!
Now 25% Less Sodium, Maintenant 25 % moins de sodium.

907 g | 64 MEATBALLS BOULETTES | FLAME BROILED CUITES SUR LE GAZ | OVEN READY PRÊTES POUR LE FOUR | KEEP FROZEN GARDER CONGELÉ

sweet and sour meatballs

MAKES: 6 SERVINGS

TIME: PREPPING 18 MINUTES, COOKING 20 MINUTES

Sweet and sour meatballs are a classic, and the green and yellow peppers in this recipe provide an additional sweetness that completes the dish. I suggest using extra-lean ground beef, but you can use any ground meat or poultry. I recommend serving it over brown rice but it is also good over whole wheat egg noodles or couscous. Serve with a side salad or steamed broccoli.

In a large bowl, combine beef, parsley, half the minced garlic, the crushed crackers and diced onion. Form meat into 24 meatballs. Set aside. Preheat oven to 425°F (220°C). In a large, lightly greased non-stick skillet over medium-high heat, sauté the rest of the minced garlic and the sliced onion for about 1 minute. Add peppers and sauté for an additional minute. Add tomato paste, tomatoes, sugar and vinegar. Slowly whisk in flour. Bring mixture to a boil, reduce heat to medium and allow to thicken. Add meatballs to skillet and allow meatballs to cook on surface without cooking all the way through. Transfer meatballs and sauce to an ovenproof dish and ensure meatballs are covered in sauce. Cover with foil and cook for 20 minutes, or until meatballs are cooked through. Remove from oven, allow to rest for 10 minutes and serve over rice.

1 LB (450 G) EXTRA-LEAN GROUND BEEF

3 TBSP (45 ML) CHOPPED FRESH PARSLEY

2 CLOVES GARLIC, MINCED

3 TBSP (45 ML) CRUSHED REDUCED-SODIUM WHOLE WHEAT CRACKERS (ABOUT 6 CRACKERS)

½ CUP (125 ML) ONION, ONE-HALF SLICED AND THE REST DICED

1 GREEN PEPPER, SEEDED AND SLICED

1 YELLOW PEPPER, SEEDED AND SLICED

¼ CUP (60 ML) PLAIN TOMATO PASTE

1 CAN (28 FL OZ/796 ML) NO-ADDED-SALT DICED TOMATOES WITH JUICE

3 TBSP (45 ML) BROWN SUGAR

3 TBSP (45 ML) VINEGAR

1 ½ TBSP (22 ML) FLOUR

3 CUPS (750 ML) COOKED BROWN RICE

MAKE IT!

SWEET AND SOUR MEATBALLS

Nutrition Facts
Per serving (4 meatballs)

Amount	% Daily Value
Calories 302	
Fat 9 g	12%
Saturated 2 g + Trans 0 g	10%
Cholesterol 64 mg	21%
Sodium 83 mg	3%
Carbohydrate 30 g	10%
Fibre 5 g	20%
Sugars 9 g	
Protein 18 g	

6%*

* Based on 1,500 mg per day, the amount recommended by Health Canada for those aged 9–50

greek meatballs with citrus mint dip 📹

MAKES: 6 SERVINGS

TIME: 20 MINUTES TOTAL

Traditional Greek keftethes are made with mint, parsley and garlic. These are a little different, but they still have that Mediterranean taste, and the citrus mint yogourt dip adds a fresh flavour. Serve them in the sauce with rice or stuffed in a pita, or as an appetizer on toothpicks with the sauce as a dip. The meat doesn't have to be ground turkey; you can also use ground chicken or extra-lean ground beef.

citrus mint dip

¾ CUP (175 ML) LOW-FAT PLAIN
   YOGOURT

1 TBSP (15 ML) CHOPPED FRESH MINT
   OR ¾ TSP (4 ML) DRIED MINT

½ RED CHILI PEPPER, FINELY CHOPPED
   (IF YOU DISLIKE SPICY FOODS, REMOVE
   SEEDS OR OMIT CHILI PEPPER)

¾ TSP (4 ML) FINELY CHOPPED LEMON
   ZEST

2 TBSP (30 ML) CRUMBLED FETA

greek meatballs

1 LB (450 G) EXTRA-LEAN GROUND
   TURKEY

2 CLOVES GARLIC, MINCED

1 SMALL ONION, MINCED

¼ CUP (60 ML) MINCED FRESH PARSLEY

2 TSP (10 ML) DRIED THYME

1 TSP (5 ML) DRIED OREGANO

1 TSP (5 ML) DRIED MINT, OR 1 TBSP
   (15 ML) FRESH MINT

A DASH OF CHILI PEPPER FLAKES

1 TSP (5 ML) WORCESTERSHIRE SAUCE

1 TSP (5 ML) LEMON ZEST, FINELY
   MINCED

2 TBSP (30 ML) CRUSHED REDUCED-
   SODIUM WHOLE WHEAT CRACKERS

1 EGG WHITE

2 TSP (10 ML) VEGETABLE OIL

For the dip:

In a small bowl, combine yogourt, mint, chili pepper, zest and feta. Set aside.

For the meatballs:

In a large bowl, combine all meatball ingredients except oil. Roll mixture into 24 meatballs. In a large non-stick skillet over medium heat, sauté meatballs in vegetable oil, turning regularly, for 8 to 10 minutes or until no longer pink in the centre.

MAKE IT!
GREEK MEATBALLS WITH CITRUS MINT DIP

Nutrition Facts
Per 6 meatballs

Amount	% Daily Value
Calories 202	
Fat 10 g	15%
Saturated 3 g + Trans 0 g	14%
Cholesterol 64 mg	21%
Sodium 217 mg	9%
Carbohydrate 8 g	3%
Fibre 1 g	3%
Sugars 3 g	
Protein 20 g	

14%*

* Based on 1,500 mg per day, the amount recommended by Health Canada for those aged 9–50

>burgers

The ever-popular burger can be adapted to anyone's preference. If "the bigger, the better" is your motto, perhaps the Triple Whopper containing 3/4 lb of beef is your fare. We all know that most burgers are not a healthy food choice.

! One beef burger with bacon and cheese can pack 1,150 mg of sodium (and 45 g of fat)!

That's almost your entire recommended amount for the day.

But "healthy" and "burger" can belong in the same sentence; just make the burgers yourself. The numbers tell it all — the recipes that follow will provide you with a burger with a sodium content ranging from only 35 mg to 155 mg. Even a prepared frozen patty, like the M&M Angus burger is going to provide far too much sodium with 410 mg packed in one patty.

For the bun, whole wheat is certainly a healthy choice. To avoid adding more sodium, you can also try half a bun, a whole wheat pita, an English muffin or half a kaiser roll.

For topping, be generous with the onion, tomato, peppers, lettuce and mushrooms, and be stingy with the store-bought ketchup, mustard, BBQ sauce, mayo, relish and pickles. Better yet, don't use store-bought at all: use our homemade ketchup (page 81), hummus (pages 39 and 40), curry mayo (page 85), tzatziki, natural peanut butter, salsa (page 51), chutney or cranberry sauce (for chicken or turkey burgers).

LES ALIMENTS
M&M
MEAT SHOPS

Thank you for inviting us to your table. We're confident that this product will meet your expectations for great taste and convenience. It's M&M's commitment to your complete satisfaction.

Nous vous remercions de nous inviter à votre table. Nous sommes assurés que la saveur et la commodité de ce produit sauront vous plaire. M&M s'engage à vous donner entière satisfaction.

M&M Finest Quality **23** Première qualité

KEEP FROZEN • GARDER CONGELÉ

Angus Beef Burgers
Burgers de bœuf Angus

Big and Juicy Burgers Made from Angus Beef!
Copieux et juteux, faits à partir de bœuf Angus !

NET 1.2 kg 2.65 lb 8 PIECES MORC.

HOLD IT!

M&M MEAT SHOPS ANGUS BURGER

Nutrition Facts
Per pattie (150 g)

Amount	% Daily Value
Calories 380	
Fat 30 g	46%
Saturated 13 g	70%
+ Trans 1 g	
Cholesterol 85 mg	28%
Sodium 410 mg	17%
Carbohydrate 5 g	2%
Fibre 0 g	0%
Sugars 0 g	
Protein 23 g	

27%*

* Based on 1,500 mg per day, the amount recommended by Health Canada for those aged 9–50

curry, lentil and sweet potato burgers

MAKES: 4 BURGERS

TIME: 15 MINUTES TOTAL

These burgers are delicious! The sweet potato is a great combination with the lentils and curry flavour. If you're not a fan of curry you can omit it completely or substitute chili powder, garlic or cayenne. I usually eat the patties by themselves but they can go into bread like a burger. I would recommend preparing your own lentils from dried, rather than using canned, but if canned is all you have on hand make sure you rinse them well and make 6 burgers, rather than 4, to cut down on the sodium content.

In a large bowl, place all ingredients except the oil. Mix until well combined and form 4 patties. Heat a large non-stick skillet or grill over medium heat. Add oil to skillet. Cook patties until browned, about 2 minutes, flip and cook other side until browned. Serve hot, topped with your favourite veggies and a dollop of curry mayo (page 85).

* TO COOK SWEET POTATO, STAB ALL OVER WITH A FORK AND MICROWAVE ON HIGH FOR 6 TO 8 MINUTES OR UNTIL TENDER.

** TO TOAST SUNFLOWER SEEDS, SAUTÉ IN A DRY PAN OVER MEDIUM-HIGH HEAT UNTIL LIGHTLY BROWNED.

1 CUP (250 mL) COOKED, PEELED AND MASHED* SWEET POTATO

1 CUP (250 mL) LENTILS, PREPARED ACCORDING TO PACKAGE (OMIT SALT)

½ CUP (125 mL) CHOPPED RED ONION

2 TBSP (30 mL) SUNFLOWER SEEDS, TOASTED**

2 TBSP (30 mL) CRUSHED LOW-SODIUM CRACKERS

¼ CUP (60 mL) ROLLED OATS

1 EGG WHITE

¼ TSP (1 mL) CUMIN

2 TSP (10 mL) CURRY POWDER

2 TSP (10 mL) CANOLA OIL

MAKE IT!
CURRY, LENTIL AND SWEET POTATO BURGERS

Nutrition Facts
Per burger

Amount	% Daily Value
Calories 212	
Fat 8 g	12%
Saturated 1 g + Trans 0 g	5%
Cholesterol 0 mg	0%
Sodium 32 mg	1%
Carbohydrate 30 g	10%
Fibre 7 g	30%
Sugars 6 g	
Protein 8 g	

2%*

* Based on 1,500 mg per day, the amount recommended by Health Canada for those aged 9–50

roasted red pepper and mushroom burgers

MAKES: 6 BURGERS

TIME: 20 MINUTES TOTAL

The roasted red pepper and mushrooms add great flavour to these burgers while replacing some of the meat with vegetables. Goat cheese, a great complement to the mushrooms and roasted red pepper, adds flavour to replace the traditional ketchup and mustard. If you're not a big fan of goat cheese, use our low-sodium ketchup (page 81), hummus (pages 39 and 40) or tzatziki sauce. These burgers contain only 142 mg of sodium.

In a medium bowl, combine meat, rolled oats, egg white, garlic, mushrooms, red pepper and pepper. Mix until well combined. With your hands, form 6 hamburger patties. Heat skillet or grill to medium, and oil lightly. Add hamburgers and cook first side until browned, about 5 minutes. Flip, and continue to cook other side until juices are clear and no pink remains in centre. Serve in pita, spreading goat cheese over top of hamburger, followed by spinach and tomato.

⅔ LB (300 G) EXTRA-LEAN HAMBURGER
   MEAT
⅓ CUP (75 ML) ROLLED OATS
1 EGG WHITE
1 CLOVE GARLIC, MINCED
8 BUTTON MUSHROOMS, DICED
1 RED PEPPER, SEEDED, ROASTED* AND
   CHOPPED
PEPPER TO TASTE
2 WHOLE WHEAT PITAS, CUT INTO
   THIRDS
4 TBSP (60 ML) SOFT GOAT CHEESE
   (2 TSP PER BURGER)
BABY SPINACH
SLICED TOMATO

* FOR DIRECTIONS ON ROASTING
   PEPPERS, SEE PAGE 40.

MAKE IT!
ROASTED RED PEPPER AND MUSHROOM BURGERS

Nutrition Facts
Per burger

Amount	% Daily Value
Calories 206	
Fat 8 g	12%
Saturated 3 g + Trans 0 g	15%
Cholesterol 37 mg	12%
Sodium 142 mg	6%
Carbohydrate 18 g	6%
Fibre 3 g	12%
Sugars 3 g	
Protein 18 g	

9%*

* Based on 1,500 mg per day, the amount recommended by Health Canada for those aged 9–50

caribbean pineapple turkey burgers

MAKES: 8 SERVINGS

TIME: 20 MINUTES TOTAL

Ginger and pineapple pair up beautifully in this turkey burger. Grilling the pineapple caramelizes the sugars and brings out the natural flavours. It's best to use fresh pineapple but you can use canned instead. Grilling the pineapple on the BBQ provides a delicious smoky flavour but if that's not an option sauté it on the stove on high heat. Good toppings for this burger include our curry mayo (page 85), homemade ketchup (page 81), citrus mint dip (page 114), or tzatziki.

In a medium bowl, combine turkey, onion, ginger, garlic, cilantro, chili flakes, pepper, breadcrumbs and egg white. With your hands, form 8 patties. Place burgers on a grill over medium heat. Place pineapple slices on grill, as well. Flip pineapple when grill marks form on side facing down and cook second side. Once pineapple is grilled, remove from BBQ or place on warming rack until burgers are cooked. Grill burgers for about 5 minutes and flip. Continue to cook until no longer pink in centre. Serve burger in 1/4 pita, topped with 1 ring of pineapple and sauce and vegetables of your choice.

1 LB (450 G) EXTRA-LEAN GROUND TURKEY

1 SMALL ONION, CHOPPED

2 TBSP (30 ML) GRATED FRESH GINGER

2 CLOVES GARLIC, MINCED

3 TBSP (45 ML) CHOPPED FRESH CILANTRO

1/2 TSP (2 ML) CHILI PEPPER FLAKES

1/2 TSP (2 ML) GROUND PEPPER

2 TBSP (30 ML) WHOLE WHEAT BREADCRUMBS

1 EGG WHITE

8 SLICES PINEAPPLE

2 WHOLE WHEAT PITAS, CUT INTO QUARTERS

MAKE IT!
CARIBBEAN PINEAPPLE TURKEY BURGERS

Nutrition Facts
Per burger

Amount	% Daily Value
Calories 174	
Fat 6 g	9%
Saturated 2 g + Trans 0 g	8%
Cholesterol 49 mg	16%
Sodium 155 mg	6%
Carbohydrate 18 g	6%
Fibre 2 g	9%
Sugars 5 g	
Protein 13 g	

10%*

* Based on 1,500 mg per day, the amount recommended by Health Canada for those aged 9–50

>shepherd's pie

Shepherd's pie is a great comfort food. It used to be regarded as a poor man's meal when potatoes were the common staple, vegetables were fresh from the garden and beef and lamb were cheap. I'd say that poor man was onto something.

You can buy a shepherd's pie already prepared and conveniently frozen. All you have to do is stick it in the oven. The downside is that it's not likely a healthy choice. It's probably high in sodium and much too high in fat.

! Check the label. One serving of a commonly available frozen shepherd's pie contains 410 mg of sodium.

That's 27 per cent of your sodium for the whole day.

Fortunately, making shepherd's pie from scratch is simple and it's a great way to use up leftovers. With a little added time in the kitchen you can enjoy it whenever you want without eating all that sodium. I've been preparing my shepherd's pie from this recipe for years, and one serving contains only 73 mg of the stuff. That's just 5 per cent of your recommended daily amount and proves how a little extra work pays off. This pie is lower in fat, too, and higher in fibre, with more vegetables and excellent flavour. Note the recipe serving size is slightly smaller than the commercial product, but it is just as satisfying.

HOLD IT!
PC BLUE MENU REDUCED FAT SHEPHERD'S PIE

Nutrition Facts
Per 1/4 pie (225 g)

Amount	% Daily Value
Calories 280	
Fat 9 g	14%
Saturated 5 g + Trans 0.4 g	27%
Cholesterol 60 mg	20%
Sodium 410 mg	17%
Carbohydrate 28 g	9%
Fibre 2 g	8%
Sugars 5 g	
Protein 22 g	

27%*

* Based on 1,500 mg per day, the amount recommended by Health Canada for those aged 9–50

shepherd's pie 📹

MAKES: 6 SERVINGS

TIME: PREPPING 20 MINUTES, COOKING 20 TO 30 MINUTES

In this recipe I cut down the sodium by using low-sodium tomato sauce and adding no salt. The texturized vegetable protein (TVP) is a healthier alternative to ground meat. TVP is made from soy, has the same texture as ground meat and really takes on the flavour of the seasonings. Even the pickiest of eaters won't complain; but you can still use extra-lean ground chicken, turkey or beef if you like.

In the recipe I recommend removing the peel from the sweet potato for appearance but I usually just mash it in with the potato, myself, for the added fibre. I also usually add a layer of cooked chopped broccoli between the TVP and potato that I omitted here to save time. Feel free to add it back, if you like. Make sure you check the labels and buy the lowest-sodium canned tomato sauce and tomato paste you can find — some brands pack quite a sodium punch.

2 CUPS (500 mL) NON-HYDRATED TEXTURIZED VEGETABLE PROTEIN (TVP, ALSO KNOWN AS SOY FLOUR)

2 MEDIUM SWEET POTATOES

1 TSP (5 mL) VEGETABLE OIL

1 MEDIUM ONION, DICED

3 CLOVES GARLIC, MINCED

1 CAN (5.5 FL OZ/175 mL) TOMATO PASTE

1 CAN (14 FL OZ/398 mL) TOMATO SAUCE

1 TBSP (15 mL) DRIED PARSLEY

½ TBSP (7 mL) DRIED BASIL

2 TSP (10 mL) CHILI PASTE

1 CUP (250 mL) FROZEN PEAS AND CARROTS, THAWED

1 CUP (250 mL) FROZEN CORN, THAWED

Place TVP in a bowl with a cover. Pour in 1 cup of boiling water, mix, cover and let rest for 8 to 10 minutes. Pierce sweet potatoes several times with a fork and microwave for 14 minutes or until soft. While sweet potatoes are cooking, heat oil in a large skillet over medium heat, add onion and garlic and sauté until fragrant, about 30 seconds. Add hydrated TVP to garlic mixture. Mix in tomato paste, tomato sauce, parsley, basil and chili paste. Mix in peas and carrots and corn. Continue to sauté for 3 to 4 minutes, until heated through. Remove sweet potatoes from microwave, peel and mash. Mix in a little water with the sweet potato to get a consistency that will spread easily. Place TVP mixture in an ovenproof dish. Spread mashed sweet potato evenly on top. Bake for 20 to 30 minutes, until heated through.

MAKE IT!
SHEPHERD'S PIE

Nutrition Facts
Per 1/6 pie (212 g)

Amount	% Daily Value
Calories 247	
Fat 3 g	4%
Saturated 0 g + Trans 0 g	2%
Cholesterol 0 mg	0%
Sodium 73 mg	3%
Carbohydrate 40 g	13%
Fibre 11 g	44%
Sugars 15 g	
Protein 21 g	

5%*

* Based on 1,500 mg per day, the amount recommended by Health Canada for those aged 9–50

>spaghetti with meat

Frozen spaghetti and meat sauce dinners seem cheap and convenient, but can be costly to your health. When you look at the nutritional label you should stick to foods with a %DV of 5% or less (115 mg) and never exceeding 10%DV (230 mg), but one package of Michelina's Spaghetti Bolognese contains 53% of your recommended daily sodium intake, and these frozen dinners are in small portions. There's a lot of sodium in those small packages!

What if you make your meat sauce from scratch, using bottled or canned tomato sauce? Unfortunately, you are still preparing a high-sodium meal.

Prego Traditional Tomato Sauce contains almost as much sodium as the already prepared meat sauces — 360 mg per 1/2 cup serving.

But you can enjoy spaghetti with meat sauce and treat your body kindly. It's very simple and quick to make a healthy version of this one-pot meal.

Cut back on that sneaky sodium by using no-added-salt canned tomatoes. Serve it over whole wheat pasta and you'll both increase your fibre intake and include 3 of the 4 food groups. This sauce won't taste bland, because it has the proper combination of spices to zest it up.

Spaghetti with a tomato meat sauce can be nutritious and quick to prepare. Spaghetti sauce freezes well, too, so your leftovers can make a quick meal or lunch for when you're on the go.

HOLD IT!
MICHELINA'S SPAGHETTI BOLOGNESE

Nutrition Facts
255 g

Amount	% Daily Value
Calories 320	
Fat 6 g	10%
Saturated 2 g + Trans 0 g	
Cholesterol 10 mg	3%
Sodium 800 mg	**33%**
Carbohydrate 52 g	17%
Fibre 4 g Sugars 5 g	16%
Protein 11 g	

53%*

* Based on 1,500 mg per day, the amount recommended by Health Canada for those aged 9–50

spaghetti and meat sauce

MAKES 8 SERVINGS

TIME: 30 MINUTES TOTAL

This sauce freezes well so your leftovers can make a quick meal or lunch to have on the go. Note that the sodium in this recipe is way less than the sodium in just the sauce if you use store-bought.

In a non-stick skillet over medium-high heat, sauté meat until no longer pink. Remove meat from skillet, place in a strainer and run under warm water to remove excess fat. In a large saucepan, heat oil over medium heat. Add garlic, onion, Italian seasoning, basil, and chili pepper flakes, and sauté until fragrant, about 30 seconds. Add zucchini and mushrooms and sauté for 3 to 4 minutes, until slightly tender. Add tomato paste and sauté for 1 minute. Add red wine and simmer for 5 minutes. Add meat to saucepan and heat through. Add tomatoes, sugar and cinnamon (if desired). Bring to a boil, stirring constantly. Decrease heat to low and simmer for 8 to 10 minutes. Serve over pasta.

1 LB (450 G) EXTRA-LEAN GROUND BEEF

1 TSP (5 ML) CANOLA OIL

6 CLOVES GARLIC, MINCED

1 MEDIUM ONION, DICED

2 TBSP (30 ML) ITALIAN SEASONING

1 TBSP (15 ML) DRIED BASIL

1/2 TSP (2 ML) CHILI PEPPER FLAKES

1 LARGE ZUCCHINI, CHOPPED

6 MEDIUM MUSHROOMS, SLICED

1 CAN (5.5 FL OZ/156 ML) TOMATO
  PASTE

1 CUP (250 ML) RED WINE

2 CANS (28 FL OZ/796 ML) NO-ADDED-
  SALT DICED TOMATOES WITH JUICE

1 TSP (5 ML) SUGAR

1/4 TSP (1 ML) CINNAMON (OPTIONAL)

6 CUPS (1.5 L) SPAGHETTI, COOKED
  ACCORDING TO PACKAGE DIRECTIONS
  (OMIT OIL AND SALT)

MAKE IT!

SPAGHETTI AND MEAT SAUCE

Nutrition Facts
Per serving (1/8 of recipe)

Amount	% Daily Value
Calories 371	
Fat 7 g	11%
Saturated 2 g + Trans 0 g	12%
Cholesterol 36 mg	12%
Sodium 83 mg	3%
Carbohydrate 55 g	18%
Fibre 10 g	41%
Sugars 12 g	
Protein 22 g	

6%*

* Based on 1,500 mg per day, the amount recommended by Health Canada for those aged 9–50

>lasagna

Lasagna makes a great meal option because it's both tasty and filling, and can be made with so many nutritious ingredients. It's truly a dish that can be made to anyone's taste. Because it is such a popular meal choice, it is also readily available in frozen varieties, even in individual serving sizes! It doesn't get much more convenient than that, but, as often happens when it comes to food, convenience comes at a cost to health. Weight Watchers Smart Ones Lasagna Florentine may seem like a wise choice, as the name implies, but it makes up 39 per cent of the daily sodium recommendation.

That's simply too much sodium!

Luckily, this home-cooked alternative contains less than a third of the sodium in the frozen option, and leftovers are just as easy to freeze and microwave later!

HOLD IT!
WEIGHT WATCHERS SMART ONES LASAGNA FLORENTINE

Nutrition Facts
Per 1 package (297 g)

Amount	% Daily Value
Calories 290	
Fat 6 g	9%
Saturated 5 g + Trans 0.3 g	27%
Cholesterol 20 mg	7%
Sodium 580 mg	**24%** 39%*
Carbohydrate 44 g	15%
Fibre 5 g	20%
Sugars 11 g	
Protein 15 g	

* Based on 1,500 mg per day, the amount recommended by Health Canada for those aged 9–50

vegetable lasagna

MAKES 8 SERVINGS

TIME: PREPPING 20 MINUTES, COOKING 50 MINUTES

This hearty dish is a delicious way to serve a variety of vegetables, and leftovers can be frozen for a convenient and healthy meal.

Preheat oven to 400°F (200°C). In a large skillet, heat oil over low-medium heat. Add garlic and onion and sauté until fragrant, about 30 seconds. Increase heat to medium, sauté eggplant, zucchini and mushrooms until slightly tender, 4 to 5 minutes. Add well-drained diced tomatoes, oregano and parsley, continue to sauté for several minutes. Add tomato sauce and spinach, sauté until the spinach is wilted and remove from burner. In a small bowl, mix ricotta cheese with egg white. Place vegetable and tomato mixture in a large bowl, add ricotta cheese and mix until well blended.

In an ovenproof dish, spread a thin layer of the vegetable sauce mixture — just enough to cover the bottom. Follow with a single layer of noodles. Top noodles with a layer of vegetable sauce, reserving about 1 cup (250 mL), and add a thin layer of fresh basil. Top vegetable sauce with remaining noodles, followed by reserved sauce. Leave uncovered and bake for 35 to 40 minutes. Sprinkle top with mozzarella cheese and continue to bake for another 10 to 15 minutes. Remove from oven and allow to rest for 10 to 15 minutes before serving.

2 TSP (10 mL) VEGETABLE OIL

5 CLOVES GARLIC, MINCED

1 ONION, CHOPPED

½ LB (230 G) EGGPLANT (ABOUT HALF A LARGE EGGPLANT)

1 LARGE ZUCCHINI, SLICED

8 MUSHROOMS, SLICED

1 CAN (28 FL OZ/796 ML) NO-ADDED-SALT DICED TOMATOES, DRAINED WELL

1 TSP (5 mL) DRIED OREGANO

3 TBSP (45 mL) CHOPPED FRESH PARSLEY

1 CAN (28 FL OZ/796 ML) NO-ADDED-SALT TOMATO SAUCE

3 CUPS (750 mL) FRESH SPINACH, WELL WASHED

1 CONTAINER (14 FL OZ/425 G) LIGHT RICOTTA, LIQUID DRAINED OFF

1 EGG WHITE

9 LASAGNA NOODLES CUT IN HALF CROSSWAYS, COOKED *al dente* (WITHOUT SALT OR OIL)

½ CUP CHOPPED FRESH BASIL

1 CUP (250 mL) GRATED LIGHT OR PART-SKIM MOZZARELLA

MAKE IT!
VEGETABLE LASAGNA

Nutrition Facts
Per serving (1/8 of dish)

Amount	% Daily Value
Calories 252	
Fat 8 g	12%
Saturated 5 g + Trans 0 g	25%
Cholesterol 27 mg	9%
Sodium 211 mg	9%
Carbohydrate 30 g	10%
Fibre 5 g	20%
Sugars 6 g	
Protein 17 g	

14%*

* Based on 1,500 mg per day, the amount recommended by Health Canada for those aged 9–50

>breaded and seasoned fish

Fish is a great source of protein and heart-healthy omega-3 fatty acids, and can take on so many flavours with a little seasoning. There are few people who can pass up breaded fish at a local pub, and frozen brands often seem a healthier alternative to this delicious meal.

Pre-seasoned or breaded frozen brands seem like a convenient choice,

! but with up to 350 mg of sodium in a single fillet, it's questionable whether this can still be considered a healthy meal option.

To put this into perspective — 350 mg sodium is 23 per cent of your recommended daily sodium intake.

However, with the recipes provided here you can get all the flavour of a seasoned fish dish and the crunch of breaded fish with only a fraction of the sodium found in these commercial brands. It may take a little more time to make, but it's easy! With fish being so versatile it's just a matter of knowing what seasonings and sauces to add to complement a particular fish. The sodium in the following recipes ranges from only 28 to 109 mg sodium and the serving size is a more appropriate 90 to 100 g. They are sure to be a catch!

HOLD IT!

HIGH LINER PAN-SEAR SELECTS
ROASTED GARLIC & HERBS HADDOCK

Nutrition Facts
Per fillet (140 g)

Amount	% Daily Value
Calories 210	
Fat 9 g	14%
Saturated 1 g + Trans 0 g	5%
Cholesterol 45 mg	15%
Sodium 350 mg	15% **23%***
Carbohydrate 11 g	4%
Fibre 1 g Sugars 0 g	4%
Protein 21 g	

* Based on 1,500 mg per day, the amount recommended by Health Canada for those aged 9–50

creamy dill salmon

MAKES: 6 SERVINGS

TIME: PREPPING 12 MINUTES, COOKING 6 TO 8 MINUTES

Most cream sauces are made with high-fat cream, but using light cream cheese and yogourt provides a delicious creamy flavoured sauce without all the added fat and sodium. This sauce is also delicious with trout.

In a small bowl, combine cream cheese, yogourt, lemon juice, dill, mustard powder and red pepper powder. Lay salmon fillets in a lightly greased pan. Top with cream sauce. Place in oven on broil for 6 to 8 minutes until salmon is cooked through and flakes easily.

¼ CUP (60 mL) LOW-FAT PLAIN CREAM CHEESE

¼ CUP (60 mL) LOW-FAT PLAIN YOGOURT

JUICE OF HALF A LEMON (ABOUT 2 TSP/10 mL)

1 TBSP (15 mL) CHOPPED FRESH DILL OR 1 TSP (5 mL) DRIED DILL

⅛ TSP (0.5 mL) MUSTARD POWDER

A PINCH OF RED PEPPER POWDER

1 LB (450 G) SALMON FILLETS

MAKE IT!
CREAMY DILL SALMON

Nutrition Facts
Per fillet (100 g)

Amount	% Daily Value
Calories 181	
Fat 12 g	18%
Saturated 3 g + Trans 0 g	16%
Cholesterol 47 mg	16%
Sodium 99 mg	4%
Carbohydrate 2 g	1%
Fibre 0 g	0%
Sugars 1 g	
Protein 17 g	

6%*

* Based on 1,500 mg per day, the amount recommended by Health Canada for those aged 9–50

mediterranean trout

MAKES: 4 SERVINGS

TIME: PREPPING 5 MINUTES, COOKING 10 MINUTES

4 TROUT FILLETS (3 OZ EACH)
2 GARLIC CLOVES, MINCED
2 TBSP (30 mL) BALSAMIC VINEGAR
1 TSP (5 mL) CHOPPED FRESH OREGANO
1 TSP (5 mL) FRESH ROSEMARY
PEPPER TO TASTE

This recipe calls for trout but you could use salmon if you prefer. The mixture of herbs provides a nice fresh flavour that is not too overpowering. You can choose to broil your fish or cook it on the grill, either way is delicious.

Place trout on a lightly greased baking sheet. Rub garlic into surface of fish. Drizzle with balsamic vinegar and top with oregano, rosemary and pepper. Broil for 10 minutes or until fish flakes easily and is cooked through.

MAKE IT!
MEDITERRANEAN TROUT

Nutrition Facts
Per fillet (90 g)

Amount	% Daily Value
Calories 110	
Fat 3 g	5%
Saturated 1 g + Trans 0 g	3%
Cholesterol 50 mg	17%
Sodium 28 mg	1%
Carbohydrate 2 g	1%
Fibre 0 g Sugars 1 g	0%
Protein 18 g	

2%*

* Based on 1,500 mg per day, the amount recommended by Health Canada for those aged 9–50

crunchy lemon haddock

MAKES: 4 SERVINGS

TIME: PREPPING 15 MINUTES, COOKING 10 TO 12 MINUTES

Panko is a Japanese breadcrumb. Most grocery stores have it now, beside the breadcrumbs. Because it is so crunchy, I thought it was deep fried until my friend Adam suggested it as a lower-sodium alternative to breadcrumbs. Was he ever right! I've actually gone a little panko-crazy now, breading everything in it, from seafood to chicken to fish. It's all delicious! If you can't find panko, use breadcrumbs or crushed low-sodium crackers.

Preheat oven to 425°F (220°C). In a medium bowl, combine buttermilk or orange juice, lemon zest and chili pepper flakes. Place haddock in buttermilk mixture, turn to coat and set aside for 10 to 15 minutes. In a flat, shallow dish, combine panko and parsley or cilantro. Remove fish from milk mixture and dredge each piece of haddock in panko mixture to coat on each side. Place on a lightly greased baking sheet. Bake for 10 to 12 minutes, or until fish flakes easily and is no longer opaque.

½ CUP (125 ML) BUTTERMILK* OR ORANGE JUICE

2 TSP (10 ML) LEMON ZEST

¾ TSP (3 ML) CHILI PEPPER FLAKES

1 LB (450 G) HADDOCK FILLETS, CUT INTO 4 EQUAL PORTIONS

½ CUP (125 ML) PANKO

2 TBSP (30 ML) CHOPPED FRESH PARSLEY OR CILANTRO

* TO MAKE BUTTERMILK SUBSTITUTE, COMBINE ½ CUP (125 ML) SKIM MILK WITH ½ TBSP (7 ML) VINEGAR AND LET SIT FOR 5 MINUTES.

MAKE IT!
CRUNCHY LEMON HADDOCK

Nutrition Facts
Per fillet

Amount	% Daily Value
Calories 140	
Fat 1 g	2%
Saturated 0 g + Trans 0 g	0%
Cholesterol 65 mg	22%
Sodium 109 mg	5%
Carbohydrate 2 g	1%
Fibre 0 g	0%
Sugars 1 g	
Protein 22 g	

8%*

* Based on 1,500 mg per day, the amount recommended by Health Canada for those aged 9–50

›fish cakes

Fish cakes are a great way to serve heart-healthy fish that even kids will enjoy. And taking only a few minutes from the freezer to the table, they provide the added bonus of convenience.

A quick glance at the nutrition labels of the most popular brands, however, makes you question the cost of this convenience.

! **High Liner Fish Cakes, which can be found in many freezers, contain 730 mg of sodium in just 2 cakes!**

And the President's Choice "healthier" Blue Menu option still contains 430 mg of sodium. Against the total daily recommended amount of 1,500, the sodium in those little fish cakes does add up!

The good news is that it is quick and easy to prepare homemade fish cakes with just 151 mg of sodium. That's a mere fraction of the amount of sodium in the commercial brands. Not only that, you can also indulge in a slightly larger serving of 3 cakes, and still be in the right range of calories and fat for a balanced meal.

HOLD IT!

HIGH LINER FISH CAKES

Nutrition Facts
Per 2 cakes (117 g)

Amount	% Daily Value
Calories 190	
Fat 6 g	9%
Saturated 0.5 g + Trans 0 g	3%
Cholesterol 20 mg	7%
Sodium 730 mg	30%
Carbohydrate 23 g	8%
Fibre 1 g	4%
Sugars 4 g	
Protein 10 g	

49%*

* Based on 1,500 mg per day, the amount recommended by Health Canada for those aged 9–50

salmon fennel cakes 📹

MAKES: 4 SERVINGS (3 CAKES EACH)

TIME: PREPPING 8 MINUTES, COOKING 15 MINUTES

Though fish cakes are usually made with fresh fish loins, to speed up preparation I use low-sodium canned salmon here. You don't need to remove the bones from canned salmon — the bones are well-cooked, and a good source of calcium. They mash up easily, but you can omit them if you like.

Wash potato and pierce all over with a fork. Cook in microwave for 6 to 8 minutes, until tender. In a medium bowl, mash salmon and bones (skin removed and discarded). In a lightly greased non-stick skillet over medium heat, sauté the green onion and diced fennel bulb for 1-2 minutes, stirring with a fork, until fennel is slightly tender. Add green onions, fennel leaves, Worcestershire sauce, mustard powder, mayo or salad dressing, hot sauce and 1 tbsp (15 mL) reserved salmon liquid (if mixture appears dry) to mashed salmon and mix until well combined. Add pepper to taste. With your hands, form salmon mixture into 12 patties about 3 inches (7.5 cm) in diameter. Dredge each patty in flour to lightly coat each side. In a larger non-stick skillet over medium-high heat, place 1/2 tbsp (7 mL) of oil. When oil is hot, add 4 salmon cakes and cook until browned, flip and continue to cook until browned on other side and heated through. Keep finished patties warm while you repeat instructions with 1/2 tbsp oil per 4 patties for the remainder.

1 LARGE POTATO

1 CAN (213 G) NO-ADDED-SALT SALMON, DRAINED BUT WITH LIQUID RESERVED

¼ CUP (60 mL) CHOPPED GREEN ONIONS (ABOUT 4 GREEN ONIONS)

½ CUP (125 mL) DICED FENNEL BULB

3 TBSP (45 mL) FRESH FENNEL LEAVES

2 TSP (10 mL) WORCESTERSHIRE SAUCE

1 TSP (5 mL) MUSTARD POWDER

2 TBSP (30 mL) LIGHT MAYO OR SALAD DRESSING

A DASH OF HOT SAUCE

FRESH GROUND PEPPER

FLOUR

1 ½ TBSP (22 mL) CANOLA OIL

MAKE IT!
SALMON FENNEL CAKES

Nutrition Facts
Per 3 cakes (158 g)

Amount	% Daily Value
Calories 218	
Fat 10 g	15%
Saturated 2 g + Trans 0 g	8%
Cholesterol 26 mg	9%
Sodium 151 mg	6%
Carbohydrate 19 g	6%
Fibre 2 g	8%
Sugars 2 g	
Protein 13 g	

10%*

* Based on 1,500 mg per day, the amount recommended by Health Canada for those aged 9–50

>seafood vegetable medley

Frozen pasta entrees are a convenient meal in a bag. Quick and easy to prepare in the microwave or on the stove, they're ideal for the busy household after a long day at work. There are plenty of different flavours to choose from too.

! But look at the nutrition labels: you may be alarmed.

These entrees are not only high in fat and calories but far too high in sodium. A half-package serving of Knorr's Shrimp, Asparagus and Penne is high in fat (21 g) and calories (470), which would be bad enough, but it also contains 1,300 mg of sodium! That is 87 per cent of your recommended daily value of sodium for the whole day. Numbers like that should definitely make you think twice.

Luckily, you can easily make your own quick and delicious convenience meals. The following garlic and basil shrimp medley requires only 20 minutes in the kitchen, tastes great and, best of all, has less than one-eighth the sodium! Need I say more?

HOLD IT!
KNORR SHRIMP, ASPARAGUS AND PENNE

Nutrition Facts
Per 1/2 package (340 g)

Amount	% Daily Value
Calories 470	
Fat 21 g	32%
Saturated 9 g + Trans 0.4 g	47%
Cholesterol 90 mg	30%
Sodium 1300 mg	54%
Carbohydrate 55 g	18%
Fibre 4 g	16%
Sugars 4 g	
Protein 16 g	

87%*

* Based on 1,500 mg per day, the amount recommended by Health Canada for those aged 9–50

garlic and basil shrimp medley

MAKES: 4 SERVINGS

TIME: 20 MINUTES TOTAL

One serving of grain, according to Canada's Food Guide, is a 1/2 cup (125 mL) of pasta. Since 1 actual serving of pasta might easily be at least 3 cups (750 mL) (especially in those pasta-heavy prepared, frozen entrees), you might be eating 6 servings of grain in one meal! So I recommend here that you limit the pasta and load up your sauce with vegetables. You can add a sprinkle of goat cheese if you like, but this dish contains a lot of flavour even without it.

Prepare the whole wheat rotini according to the package instructions (omitting any oil and salt). Heat the oil in a large skillet over medium heat, and sauté the garlic and onion for 30 seconds. Add zucchini and tomatoes and continue to cook, stirring regularly, until tomatoes burst, about 8 to 10 minutes. Add shrimp and cook for about 2 minutes until shrimp is almost cooked. Stir in basil and cooked rotini and continue to cook until mixed and heated through. Serve topped with goat cheese (optional) and pepper.

4 CUPS (1 L) WHOLE WHEAT ROTINI, PREPARED

2 TBSP (30 mL) OLIVE OIL

5 CLOVES GARLIC, MINCED

1 MEDIUM ONION, CHOPPED

2 MEDIUM ZUCCHINI, CUT LENGTHWISE INTO 3-INCH (7.6 CM) STICKS

1 PINT (475 mL) GRAPE TOMATOES

12 OZ (375 G) RAW SHRIMP, PEELED, TAILS REMOVED

3 TBSP (45 mL) CHOPPED FRESH BASIL

¼ CUP (60 mL) CRUMBLED GOAT CHEESE (OPTIONAL)

PEPPER TO TASTE

MAKE IT!
GARLIC AND BASIL SHRIMP MEDLEY

Nutrition Facts
Per serving (1/4 of recipe)

Amount	% Daily Value
Calories 430	
Fat 11 g	17%
Saturated 2 g + Trans 0 g	8%
Cholesterol 129 mg	43%
Sodium 141 mg	6%
Carbohydrate 59 g	20%
Fibre 9 g	36%
Sugars 6 g	
Protein 29 g	

10%*

* Based on 1,500 mg per day, the amount recommended by Health Canada for those aged 9–50

>hamburger and tuna helper

Betty Crocker came up with the "Helper" line more than 30 years ago. The one-skillet meals, targeted towards busy families that need quick-fix dinners, were an instant success, and with success came expansion of the original line and alternatives from the competition. Now there are so many different versions you could easily have a different "Helper" meal every night of the month.

Such a quick and convenient meal — can it be healthy too? Is that too much to hope? Sadly, yes.

! The sodium content in these products is massive.

With one-fifth of a prepared Tuna Helper package meal (about 1 cup/250 mL) you eat 680 mg of sodium. That's 45% of the recommended daily value for those aged 9-50.

I'm proud to say that I've come up with an alternative. This recipe is delicious, packed with potassium, lower in fat, higher in protein and much lower in sodium. I will admit, though, I had my doubts when I first attempted to come up with one. The biggest challenge was how to prepare a tasty dish without the cheese and the high-fat cream sauce. But perseverance pays. It may take you a little longer to prepare this meal than to whip up a Helper version, but it's worth it. I've kicked 508 mg of sodium to the curb here and you won't even miss it. A serving of this tuna casserole contains only 172 mg.

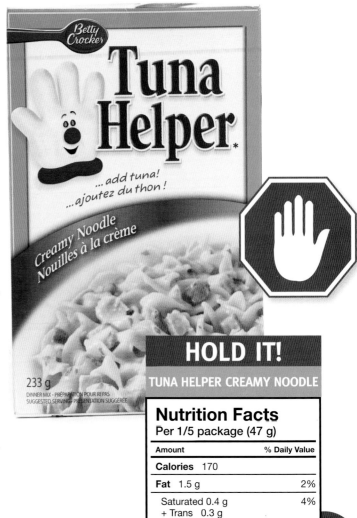

HOLD IT!
TUNA HELPER CREAMY NOODLE

Nutrition Facts
Per 1/5 package (47 g)

Amount	% Daily Value
Calories 170	
Fat 1.5 g	2%
Saturated 0.4 g + Trans 0.3 g	4%
Cholesterol 0 mg	0%
Sodium 680 mg	28%
Carbohydrate 34 g	11%
Fibre 1 g Sugars 2 g	5%
Protein 5 g	

45%*

* Based on 1,500 mg per day, the amount recommended by Health Canada for those aged 9–50

sweet potato and spinach tuna casserole

MAKES 8 SERVINGS

TIME: PREPPING 20 MINUTES, COOKING 20 MINUTES

Traditional tuna casserole uses cheddar cheese and cream of mushroom soup, but both are high in sodium. The tasty alternative here is a low-fat mushroom roux and lots of vegetables to add flavour. If you're not a big fan of tuna, you can either make it vegetarian or replace the tuna with diced cooked chicken, flaked cooked salmon, shrimp or scallops. Panko is a Japanese breadcrumb that provides little sodium but a great crunchy texture.

Preheat oven to 400°F (200°C). In a medium non-stick saucepan, melt margarine over medium heat and add garlic. Sauté until fragrant, about 30 seconds. Reduce heat to low, add milk and slowly add flour while whisking constantly. Add mushrooms and onion powder and continue to stir. Once sauce has slightly thickened, add cream cheese and Parmesan and continue to stir until melted. Add pepper to taste. Set saucepan aside and cover. In a large non-stick skillet over medium-high heat, fry onion and broccoli for 3 to 4 minutes. Add spinach and cook, stirring, until wilted. In a large bowl, combine noodles, sweet potato, cooked vegetables and mashed tuna. Pour in the sauce and mix until well combined. Pour mixture into a 8 x 11 1/2 in (20 x 29 cm) casserole dish. Top with panko. Bake uncovered for 20 minutes.

1 TBSP (15 ML) NON-HYDROGENATED MARGARINE
2 CLOVES GARLIC, MINCED
2 CUPS (500 ML) SKIM MILK
2 TBSP (30 ML) FLOUR
3/4 CUP (175 ML) SLICED MUSHROOMS
1 TSP (5 ML) ONION POWDER
3 TBSP (45 ML) LIGHT PLAIN CREAM CHEESE
2 TBSP (30 ML) GRATED PARMESAN
PEPPER TO TASTE
1 CUP (250 ML) DICED ONION
1 HEAD BROCCOLI, CHOPPED
2 CUPS (500 ML) SPINACH
2 CUPS (500 ML) GRATED SWEET POTATO
3 CUPS (750 ML) WHOLE WHEAT NOODLES, PREPARED ACCORDING TO PACKAGE DIRECTIONS (OMITTING ANY OIL OR SALT)
2 CANS (6 FL OZ/120 G) NO-ADDED-SALT TUNA, DRAINED AND MASHED INTO SMALLER CHUCKS
1/2 CUP (125 ML) PANKO

MAKE IT!
SWEET POTATO AND SPINACH TUNA CASSEROLE

Nutrition Facts
Per serving (1/8 of dish)

Amount	% Daily Value
Calories 229	
Fat 5 g	8%
Saturated 1 g + Trans 0 g	5%
Cholesterol 29 mg	10%
Sodium 172 mg	7%
Carbohydrate 26 g	9%
Fibre 7 g	28%
Sugars 8 g	
Protein 20 g	

11%*

* Based on 1,500 mg per day, the amount recommended by Health Canada for those aged 9–50

>pizza

Pizza is a world-wide favourite. It is convenient with its delicious crust, topped with your favourite fixings and smothered in gooey cheese. Pizza has gone beyond the traditional pepperoni and cheese from the pizza shop and taken on a much fancier flair, being served in high-end restaurants with an endless number of ingredients.

What satisfies your taste buds does not necessarily satisfy your health. It likely comes as no surprise that pizza is loaded with sodium and fat. This comes from the cheese, processed meats, pizza crust and sauce. Whether you grab a slice at the pizza shop or pop a frozen one in the oven, both options are going to provide you with far too much fat and sodium. A serving of frozen pizza like McCain Traditional Crust Deli Lovers provides not only 330 calories per pizza and 5 g of saturated but a whopping 880 mg of sodium!

That's over half your sodium for the day!

You shouldn't have to deprive yourself of pizza if you're concerned about your health. Pizza can easily be made delicious and healthy. Whenever I make pizza I always load up on veggies and choose ingredients packed with flavour to take the place of some of the cheese and processed meats. Making homemade pizza does require more time than the convenience options but I assure you once you taste them, it will be well worth the extra time. This is not to mention the homemade pizzas on the following pages contain only 236 to 306 mg of sodium and you still satisfy that pizza craving!

HOLD IT!
McCAIN TRADITIONAL CRUST DELI LOVERS PIZZA

Nutrition Facts
Per 1/4 pizza (135 g)

Amount	% Daily Value
Calories 330	
Fat 12 g	18%
Saturated 5 g + Trans 0.2 g	26%
Cholesterol 30 mg	10%
Sodium 880 mg	**37%**
Carbohydrate 39 g	13%
Fibre 2 g	8%
Sugars 3 g	
Protein 15 g	

59%*

* Based on 1,500 mg per day, the amount recommended by Health Canada for those aged 9–50

thin-crust pizza dough

MAKES: DOUGH FOR 1 PIZZA

TIME: 10 MINUTES

All good things have got to start somewhere, and pizza starts with perfect dough for the perfect crust.

In a medium bowl, combine flour, sugar and baking powder. Add margarine and stir just until a crumble is formed. Add milk and mix until just combined. Dough will be sticky. On a floured surface, knead 8 to 10 times. Spread dough on a lightly greased 9-in (23-cm) pizza pan.

1 CUP (250 mL) WHOLE WHEAT FLOUR
1 ½ TBSP (22 mL) SUGAR
2 TSP (10 mL) BAKING POWDER
3 TBSP (45 mL) NON-HYDROGENATED MARGARINE
⅓ CUP (75 mL) SKIM MILK

MAKE IT!
THIN-CRUST PIZZA DOUGH

Nutrition Facts
Per 1/6 of crust

Amount	% Daily Value
Calories 114	
Fat 4 g	5%
Saturated 1 g + Trans 0 g	5%
Cholesterol 0 mg	0%
Sodium 158 mg	7%
Carbohydrate 19 g	6%
Fibre 2 g	10%
Sugars 3 g	
Protein 3 g	

11%*

* Based on 1,500 mg per day, the amount recommended by Health Canada for those aged 9–50

pizza sauce

MAKES: APPROX. 1 3/4 CUPS (400 mL)

TIME: 5 MINUTES

1 CAN (5.5 FL OZ/156 mL) PLAIN
   TOMATO PASTE
1 CUP (250 mL) WATER
2 CLOVES GARLIC, MINCED
1 TSP (5 mL) DRIED OREGANO
½ TSP (2 mL) DRIED BASIL
¼ TSP (1 mL) DRIED ROSEMARY
1 TSP (5 mL) ONION POWDER

Tomato pastes vary significantly in sodium content, and the flavoured versions like "herb and garlic" contain a lot more sodium than the plain. Check the labels, buy the plain paste with the lowest sodium, and add your own herbs and spices.

In a small bowl, combine all ingredients.

MAKE IT!
PIZZA SAUCE

Nutrition Facts
Per 2 tbsp (30 mL)

Amount	% Daily Value
Calories 23	
Fat 0 g	0%
Saturated 0 g	0%
+ Trans 0 g	
Cholesterol 0 mg	0%
Sodium 25 mg	1%
Carbohydrate 5 g	2%
Fibre 1 g	4%
Sugars 3 g	
Protein 1 g	

2%*

* Based on 1,500 mg per day, the amount recommended by Health Canada for those aged 9–50

mediterranean veggie pizza

MAKES: 6 SERVINGS (2 SLICES EACH)

TIME: PREPPING 20 MINUTES, COOKING 15 TO 18 MINUTES

Pizza doesn't need to be buried in pepperoni and cheese to be delicious; this combination of veggies and goat cheese provides lots of flavour.

Preheat oven to 400°F (200°C). Spread pizza sauce over an uncooked 9-in (23-cm) pizza dough (page 137). Dress pizza with red peppers, spinach, zucchini, green onion and avocado. Top with crumbled goat cheese. Bake for 15 to 18 minutes, until the crust is browned and crispy.

PIZZA DOUGH (PAGE 137)

PIZZA SAUCE (PAGE 138)

2 ROASTED RED PEPPERS*, SEEDED AND CHOPPED

2 CUPS (250 ML) CHOPPED SPINACH

1 ZUCCHINI, SLICED AND CUT INTO QUARTERS

5 GREEN ONIONS, CHOPPED

HALF AN AVOCADO, THINLY SLICED

¼ CUP (60 ML) CRUMBLED GOAT CHEESE

* FOR DIRECTIONS ON ROASTING PEPPERS, SEE PAGE 40.

MAKE IT!
MEDITERRANEAN VEGGIE PIZZA

Nutrition Facts	
Per 1/6 pizza	
Amount	**% Daily Value**
Calories 223	
Fat 12 g	18%
Saturated 3 g + Trans 0 g	17%
Cholesterol 8 mg	3%
Sodium 236 mg	10%
Carbohydrate 26 g	9%
Fibre 6 g	23%
Sugars 7 g	
Protein 7 g	

16%*

...1,500 mg per day, the amount recommended by Health Canada for those aged 9–50

pineapple chicken pizza

MAKES: 6 SERVINGS (2 SLICES EACH)

TIME: PREPPING 20 MINUTES, COOKING 15 TO 18 MINUTES

PIZZA DOUGH (PAGE 137)

PIZZA SAUCE (ENTIRE YIELD OF RECIPE
ON PAGE 138)

8 OZ (250 G) COOKED CHICKEN BREAST,
SLICED

1 GREEN PEPPER, THINLY SLICED

8 MUSHROOMS, THINLY SLICED

1 SMALL ONION, THINLY SLICED

1 CUP (250 ML) PINEAPPLE TIDBITS

1 CUP (250 ML) GRATED LIGHT
MOZZARELLA

The sodium content in this pizza is slightly high and this is mostly due to the mozzarella cheese. It's best to enjoy a smaller piece or just take extra caution with your sodium intake for the rest of the day. This pizza is good with or without the chicken. Cooking the chicken does take a bit more time, unless you happen to have some already cooked on hand.

Preheat oven to 400°F (200°C). Spread pizza sauce over an uncooked 9-in (23-cm) pizza dough. Dress pizza with sliced chicken, green pepper, mushrooms, onion and pineapple. Top with mozzarella. Bake for 15 to 18 minutes, until the crust is browned and crispy.

MAKE IT!
PINEAPPLE CHICKEN PIZZA

Nutrition Facts
Per 1/6 pizza

Amount	% Daily Value
Calories 241	
Fat 9 g	14%
Saturated 3 g + Trans 1 g	14%
Cholesterol 31 mg	10%
Sodium 306 mg	13% 20%*
Carbohydrate 26 g	9%
Fibre 4 g	15%
Sugars 8 g	
Protein 16 g	

* Based on 1,500 mg per day, the amount recommended by Health Canada for those aged 9–50

Index

More delicious low-salt options!

Here are more tasty alternatives for Canadians who have to worry about high blood pressure – using the widely-recommended Dietary Approach to Stop Hypertension (DASH) which is proven to work just as well as medication. These Formac cookbooks feature quick and easy, great-tasting recipes combining fresh fruits and vegetables with a reduction in salt and sodium.

Hold the Salt!

50+ quick & easy recipes to help you eliminate salt from your diet!
Maureen Tilley

Here's help for anyone who wants easy-to-prepare recipes which are healthy, tasty and low in salt/sodium. More people are learning the benefits of low-salt eating, a proven way to reduce high blood pressure without relying on medication. This full-colour cookbook focuses on recipes that are quick, easy, and follow the DASH approach. The recipes are based on dishes from fine restaurants across Canada, with modifications where needed. Preparation time for every dish is 20 minutes or less.

This book helps make it easy and appealing to follow the DASH approach. DASH (Dietary Approach to Stop Hypertension) was developed by independent health researchers in the US who proved through two extensive research trials that this low-salt diet featuring lots of fruits and vegetables was as effective as drugs in lowering blood pressure. The diet they developed is now recommended by many health professionals in Canada and internationally.

ISBN-13: 978-0-88780-867-8, paper, $24.95
8 ¼" x 9", 96 pages, full-colour photographs, 2009 publication

Delicious DASH Flavours

The proven, drug-free, doctor-recommended approach to reducing high blood pressure

Sandra Nowlan

Written by award-winning cook and food scientist Sandra Nowlan, *Delicious DASH Flavours* is a full-colour cookbook that shows how to follow a proven, drug-free method of reducing and controlling high blood pressure. Sandra has selected delicious recipes from Canada's top chefs, which she has modified to reduce fat, cholesterol and salt while maintaining all the delectable flavour.

These recipes and suggested menus follow the guidelines of the DASH diet. DASH, which stands for Dietary Approaches to Stop Hypertension, is a diet developed through studies initiated by the U.S. National Institutes of Health. It has been proven in extensive clinical trials to be as effective as medication in lowering blood pressure. DASH emphasizes a wholesome, balanced diet low in fat and sodium and high in potassium.

ISBN-13: 978-0-88780-766-4, paper, $29.95
8 ¼" x 9", 160 pages, full-colour photographs

Low-Salt DASH Dinners

Sandra Nowlan

More and more doctors and health professionals are telling their patients that reducing salt/sodium will contribute to lower blood pressure and better health. Often they recommend the DASH approach as a great alternative to drug treatment for hypertension. For two years, they've been recommending Sandra Nowlan's path-breaking book which shows how tasty and appealing the DASH diet can be. Now Sandra Nowlan is back with a collection of recipes for simple, quick-to-prepare and tasty dinner dishes.

DASH is an alternative to drugs for anyone experiencing hypertension. Following the DASH approach, which stands for Dietary Approach to Stop Hypertension, was demonstrated to have the same impact on blood pressure as the pharmaceutical industry's medications. Health professionals who are aware of the DASH research findings are DASH's strongest advocates, and thousands of Canadians now benefit from following this approach.

ISBN-13: 978-0-88780-940-8, paper, $24.95
ISBN-13: 978-0-88780-942-2, ebook, $19.95
8 ¼" x 9", 160 pages, full-colour photographs, 2010 publication